What some have sai
Haikus and Other Po
terrenales y otros poemas by Francisco X. Alarcón

Since the late 70's when I first met Francisco, he has been sculpting his Roots poetics and mapping his travels to literary, cultural and people's centers in the Américas. This is that travelogue. It is filled with the openness of spirit wings, of Chican@ Floricanto revolutionary poetics for social change and most of all, it is flourishing with incandescent love chants and calligrams that all can read, hold up to the sun, and bow to humanity. It is the *Yolteotl,* the divine heart, the Toltecs heralded as the core of the true artist of the people. I see this collection as the mind-path for our times. A groundbreaking text and rising inspiration fountain.
— Juan Felipe Herrera, California Poet Laureate

Borderless Butterflies: Earth Haikus and Other Poems / Mariposas sin fronteras: Haikus terrenales y otros poemas is a remarkable collection, where "all of a sudden/landscapes become poems – and the road is a page," where every poet is "but a single/letter of this immense poem/called 'the universe.'" Alarcón is a master of architectural poetry. The book is divided into four main sections, one for each of the elements, the four annual cycles of nature, and the four stages of life. Some poems are designed as columns of short stanzas that can be read in any of the four directions and combinations thereof. In the midst of this complex architecture, Alarcón's poems are as minimal and vital as drops of water and light distilled by fire to their purest potency. The poet's voice is fueled by "an honesty so fierce/no ceasing till it gets/at the naked truth." Words like seeds fall to the fertile earth. Green springs again to nestle the fragile egg. It feeds the insatiable caterpillar's desire to dream in its time capsule of becoming a winged companion to the wind, oblivious to borders and frontiers. To finally fulfill the promise of life: "a new beginning/a cycle of (universal) hope." ¡Enhorabuena, Francisco X. Alarcón!
— Lucha Corpi, author of *Palabras de mediodía / Noon Words*

Francisco X. Alarcón's newest book is a silken thread strung with poems that bump up against one another, creating tremors of electricity, a litany of the brown peoples and poets of the Americas, dedications to those who have fought and are still fighting for justice and peace. Alarcón traverses borders, but his heart resides in California

where the green is like no other, an agricultural masterpiece made by the creator and tended by brown human hands. His metaphor is the monarch butterfly, "the ultimate, borderless migrant" who is beaten down with "heartless fists" only to transform and rise again. A few of my favorite lines: "in absolute calm/poets carry deep inside/a hurricane"; "somewhere/other eyes stare in awe/at the universe"; and "I burn my ships/with no way back now – ..."
> – Dorianne Laux, author of *Facts about the Moon*

"Hearts are drums." Deceptively simple, this is vintage Alarcón. All throughout *Borderless Butterflies: Earth Haikus and Other Poems / Mariposas sin fronteras: Haikus terrenales y otros poemas* he confirms what I've come to believe: he has forged one of the most exquisite poetics of minimalism in American poetry these past thirty years. But what distinguishes Alarcón is that he insists on what I'll call an indigenous spirituality that makes no distinction between animal (including humans), vegetable, and mineral – but still staying true to his activist sensibility, making music in poems that are both metaphor/image-rich ("droplets in clouds/join hands and let go/falling as rain") *and* discursive ("you risked your lives/in poems – choosing/truth over lies"), all the while deploying that signature brevity – a spare, distilled poetry where words are moss-covered stones cobbled together: a trail I've been treading since I was a teenager in San Francisco in the early 1980s.
> – Francisco Aragón, Director of Letras Latinas, Institute for Latino Studies, University of Notre Dame

Though Francisco X. Alarcón's *Borderless Butterflies: Earth Haikus and Other Poems / Mariposas sin fronteras: Haikus terrenales y otros poemas* is in praise of everywhere and all that is possible in the future, his mastery of the haiku and tanka forms is so completely a part of the reading of this beautiful book that one can't help but feel that it is a deep tribute to the Japanese people, as the victims of the Fukushima disaster, in a great solidarity from the Latino world.
> – Jack Hirschman, former Poet Laureate of San Francisco

Borderless Butterflies:
Earth Haikus and Other Poems

Mariposas sin fronteras:
Haikus terrenales y otros poemas

by

FRANCISCO X. ALARCÓN

Poetic Matrix Press

Front cover image by Joel Sartore:
"Joel Sartore/joelsartore.com"
Joel Sartore is a photographer, speaker, author, teacher, and a 20-year contributor to *National Geographic Magazine*. Monarch Butterflies were photographed In Sierra Chincua Reserve, Mexico and appeared in *National Geographics Magazine* in November 2010, Mystery of Great Migrations.

Photo of Francisco X. Alarcón on the book back cover taken on the outskirts of Tucson, Arizona by Carlos Díaz Todd.

Poetic Matrix Press
www.poeticmatrix.com

Acknowledgments

The following poems were first published in the following journals and anthologies: "For the Capitol Nine" in *El Tecolote*, July 28–August 10, 2010, Vol. 40, No. 15, San Francisco, California: 11; "Whale Songs" in *ZYZZYVA: The Last Word: West Coast Writers & Artists*, Volume XXVI, Number 3, Fall 2010: 127–129; "En invierno / In Winter," "La noche / Night," *The Acentos Poetry Review*, New York City, November 2011; "¿Qué es un poeta / What Is a Poet" in *Letras Latinas Blog*, University of Notre Dame, Monday, February 21, 2011; "Night," "Lightning," "Leaf," selected as Editor's Choice and published both in English and Hindi in *Kritya Poetry Journal*, January, 2012, India; "Estrellas / Stars" *Occupy SF: Poems from the Movement*, in Jambu Press, San Francisco, California, 2012: 93; "Self-Questions for Possible Suspects under Section 2(B) of Arizona SB 1070" in *World Literature Today*, November/December 2012: 59; "Whale Songs," Floricanto Issue edited by Francisco Aragón, *Beltway Poetry Quarterly*, Volume 13:1, Winter 2012, Washington, DC; "Poetas puentes / Bridge Poets," "El tiempo ha llegado / The Time Has Come," "Bendiciones / Blessings" in *Frontera/Esquina: Revista Mensual de Poesía*, Marzo 2013, Tijuana, Baja California; "California Green / California verde" in *Red Wheelbarrow Literary Magazine*, Volume 14, 2013: 46–49; "Desert Altar / Altar del desierto" in *Pilgrimage: Story, Spirit, Witness, Place*, Volume 38, Issue 1, 2014: 63–65; "Yolanda – Senryu," "Yolanda – Haiku," "Filipino Sun – Haiga," and "Filipino Hay(Na)ku" in *Surges: Outpourings in Haiyan/Yolanda's Wake*, edited by Rosana B. Golez and Joel P. Garduce, Manila, Philippines, 2013: 58–60; "Fruitful Eden / Fructífero Edén" in *Feather Floating on the Water: Poems for our Children*, edited by Virginia Barrett, Jambu Press, San Francisco, 2014: 60–62; "América": 140; and "Bendiciones / Blessings": 155. "García Lorca–Tanka" and "Poema / Poem" in *Merced River Literary Review*, Volume 1, Merced College, 2014: 4–5.

Many of the poems included in *Borderless Butterflies:Earth Haikus and Other Poems / Mariposas sin fronteras: Haikus terrenales y otros poemas* were first posted on the Facebook page "Poets Responding to SB 1070" that was created by the author in May 2010 in response to the anti-immigrant Arizona law SB 1070. The author wants to thank all the poets who have served as moderators of this Facebook page and who are listed here in alphabetic order: Carmen Calatayud, Lorna Dee Cervantes, Elena Díaz Bjorkquist, Antoniette Nora Clayton, Sonia Gutiérrez, Israel Francisco Haros López, José Hernández Díaz, Andrea

Hernández Holm, Scott Maurer, Edith Morris-Vásquez, Abel Salas, Raúl Sánchez, Hedy García Treviño, Alma Luz Villanueva, and Meg Withers. The poet also wants to acknowledge two new moderators of this page who have also been active participants since its inception: Iris de Anda and Sharon Elliott. Some of these poems were also posted on the On-Line Floricanto of "La Bloga" edited by Michael Sedano.

The author wants to give special thanks to Arturo Mantecón for reviewing the English version of the poems and to Graciela B. Ramírez for doing the same for the Spanish version. The poet also wants to acknowledge the support of Poetic Matrix Press: James Downs, Associate Editor, John Patterson, Publisher, and Devon Patterson who headed the Indiegogo campaign to fund this book project. Finally, the author wants to express his gratitude to filmmaker Manuela Vargas Fernández for the wonderful videos featuring the poet reading from *Borderless Butterflies: Earth Haikus and Other Poems / Mariposas sin fronteras: Haikus terrenales y otros poemas.*

Dedications

to Nina Serrano and Odilia Galván Rodríguez,
fellow poet travellers on this poetry journey

and Javier Pinzón, who has always made this life
journey a true pleasure in full love

– Francisco X. Alarcón

be the change
you want to see
in the world

sé el cambio
que deseas ver
en el mundo

– Mahatma Gandhi

Contents

Borderless Butterflies:
Earth Haikus and Other Poems

Mariposas sin fronteras:
Haikus terrenales y otros poemas

I Tierra / Earth
   Poemas y mariposas... / Poems and Butterflies...

II Fuego / Fire
Batiendo oscuras... / Striking Dark...

III Agua / Water
Gotas en nubes... / Droplets in Clouds...

IV Aire / Air
El aleteo... / The Wing Flapping...

Que mariposas... / May butterflies...

About Francisco
Press Producers

Foreword

Borderless Butterflies: Earth Haikus and Other Poems / Mariposas sin fronteras: Haikus terrenales y otros poemas by Francisco X. Alarcón is a book of poems for the earth and the people, crafted by a poet at the peak of his power. It speaks to the porousness of our boundaries, and the futility of all attempts to separate people and regions so intimately intertwined. Alarcón is a man who, like the monarch butterfly he eulogizes, lives in and migrates between many worlds. From Los Angeles to Guadalajara, from the Mission barrio in San Francisco to Stanford and UC Davis, he has lived fully immersed in the diverse cultural landscape of California and Mexico.

Prevalent in Alarcón's works, as Francisco Aragón states in his insightful blurb, is "an indigenous spirituality that makes no distinction between animal (including humans), vegetable, and mineral." Without a doubt Francisco is inspired by his Mesoamerican heritage and poets like Nezahualcoyotl. He is inspired also by the Sufi mystic poet Rumi, the mystic poets of the Golden Age in Spain as well as by Federico García Lorca and more contemporary poets – revolutionary poet Roque Dalton of El Salvador and groundbreaking Chicana poet/essayist Gloria Anzaldúa. But the *haiku, senryu,* and *tanka* forms of the Japanese poetic tradition give shape to many of his "winged poems," the meta-poetic butterflies of this collection that come to Francisco so effortlessly.

This is a work of rare beauty and intelligence. Through *tierra, fuego, agua,* and *aire,* Alarcón takes us on a journey into our own psyche and through the concerns of our world – immigration and identity, the fragility and strength of our natural environment, the many faces of love, and the politics of a world in great need of illumination. Through everything he gives voice to our own unspoken feelings, and does so with delicate yet powerful language. His language is lean and brief; his poems puncture the skin and pierce the heart. These poems are a constant source of wisdom and grace.

In these pages Francisco recapitulates the last 50 years; the struggles of so many, the dreams and the actions of millions seeking to emerge from a world that has been compromised. The four poems, *América,* shout it out in four languages; English, Spanish, Irish and Dutch: from *América*

booming loud and bright:
"I'm your country too"
this Fourth of July
•••

con estrueno y luz:
"yo soy tu nación también
este Cuatro de Julio"

• • •

glé os ard an liú:
'Is mise do thírse chomh maith'
an Ceathrú Lá d'Iúil

• • •

knallend luid en hel
"Ik ben ook jouw land"
op deze vierde juli

We are all here from many places and we are this América.

But it is not enough to shout it out. The poet is a voice indeed,
but the poets voice has a purpose: from *"¿Qué es un poeta?"* and
"What Is A Poet?"

a lamp	an unending gaze	a butterfly flitting
that burns	keeping vigil over	a hummingbird hovering–
from dusk to dawn	the fate of others	here but never bound

a voiceless voice	an honesty so fierce –	when a poet dies
that is at once joy	no ceasing till it gets	his poems unfurl
and rage	at the naked truth	inside our chest

• • •

una lámpara	una mirada	una mariposa
encendida durante	que no deja de velar	un colibrí en el aire –
toda la noche	por los demás	un ser y no estar

una voz sin voz	una honestidad	cuando un poeta muere
que es alegría y	tan feroz hasta dejar	sus poemas florecen
enojo a la vez	desnuda a la verdad	en nuestro corazón

Poetry is beauty and truth. We are caught up in both and then,
and together, there is love. Let us not be maudlin, it is love. The love of
the earth, the love of the people, the love of this life, and it is for everyone,
no one – no one – is left out. Francisco calls to us again and again in these
pages and the monarch butterfly is his symbol, his lens to let us see. The
monarch butterfly has a unique mission, it migrates across all borders in
its quest for life; its future is in jeopardy, but it continues its journey and
calls out to us with its beauty to wake up and see what we are doing, and

help them in their on-going journey of life. It is like that for all of us Francisco assures us. We all have this mission to assist each other, to not turn our backs on those in need.

Living Targets

given away
by the dark tone

of our skin
the flapping

colorful birds
in our tongue

we are here
walking suspects

living targets
always free

as breathing air
in the loving arms

of each other

July 15, 2013

      Ultimately this is a renewal, a new call to continue, to not let go of the beauty of past efforts, there is more to be done, new voices to be heard; new poems and new songs for another generation. New tears to be shed for all of us who are lost, in pain, in need.

somos solo una	we are but a single
letra del poema inmenso	letter of this immense poem
llamado "universo"	called "the universe"

      Read *Borderless Butterflies: Earth Haikus and Other Poems / Mariposas sin fronteras: Haikus terrenales y otros poemas* again and again. There are moments you will be brought to tears realizing, through Francisco's words, the beauty of this earth and what beautiful people we are.

      – John Peterson, Publisher

Borderless Butterflies:
Earth Haikus and Other Poems

Mariposas sin fronteras:
Haikus terrenales y otros poemas

I Tierra / Earth

poemas y mariposas
con alas sobrevuelan
cualquier frontera

poems and butterflies
have wings to fly over any
border and divide

Haikus terrenales

poema primordial –
el latido maternal
de nueve meses

21 de marzo de 2011

la noche – taza
de café vertida sobre
el mantel terrenal

4 de julio de 2011

súbitamente
los paisajes son poemas
y el camino es página

4 de enero de 2012

si un árbol cae
¿quién lo lee? – el mejor
libro aún es árbol

7 de febrero de 2012

todos somos hojas
temblando, cayendo
de un baobab de África

17 de marzo de 2012

flores / cantos
canto flores –
floricantos

Earth Haikus

primordial poem –
the maternal heartbeat
of nine months

March 21, 2011

the night – a cup
of black coffee poured over
the Earth's tablecloth

July 4, 2011

all of a sudden
landscapes become poems
and the road is a page

January 4, 2012

if a tree should fall
who will read it? – the greatest
book is yet a tree

February 7, 2012

we all are leaves
trembling, falling from
an African baobab

March 17, 2012

flowers / songs
song flowers –
flowersongs

girasol
Sol Flor
floricanto Sol

Sol / Luna / luz
Luz lunar
Luz solar

por amor a la Luna
luciérnagas dan luz
en la oscuridad

todos somos uno –
¿somos todos uno?
uno todos somos

26 de marzo de 2012

somos solo una
letra del poema inmenso
llamado "universo"

9 de junio de 2012

"mi telaraña ata
Punta Seattle y el Monte
Rainer" – Poeta Araña

Seattle, Washington
13 de junio de 2012

los poetas son
mariposas migrantes
de la palabra

los poetas son
naguales transformando
sueños en realidad

sunflower
Flower Sun
Sun flowersong

Sun / Moon / light
Moonlight
Sunlight

twinkling fireflies
in love with the Moon
swirl in the night sky

we all are one –
are we all one?
one we all are

March 26, 2012

we are but a single
letter of this immense poem
called "the universe"

June 9, 2012

"my silk web bonds
Seattle Space Needle and Mount
Rainer" – Spider Poet

Seattle, Washington
June 13, 2012

poets are
migrant butterflies
of the word

poets are
naguales transforming
dreams into reality

los poetas son
curanderos seguidores
de los colibríes

poets are
healers – disciples
of hummingbirds

los poetas en
soledad dan aliento
a la hermandad

poets in their
solitude give breath
to brotherhood

20 de octubre de 2012

October 20, 2012

poesía – magia
en acción – el poeta –
chamán de la palabra

poetry – magic
in action – the poet –
a word shaman

26 de noviembre de 2012

November 26, 2012

credo de poeta –
entre menos
más

poet's creed –
from less
more

la poesía habla
aun en el silencio
más total

poetry speaks
even in complete
silence

poesía –
el agua que fluye;
poema – el vaso

poetry –
the flowing water;
poem – the glass

vasto mar – silencio
hecho canto hondo
de ballenas-poetas

vast sea – silence
stirring soulful wails
of whales-poets

todo solo
junto al Sol y el mar –
todo es uno

all alone
by the Sun and sea –
all is one

pongo una concha
al oído – oigo el mar
escucho a Rumi

I put a seashell
to my ear – I hear the sea
listen to Rumi

en calma absoluta
los poetas llevan dentro
un huracán

parada sola
una palmera ante un huracán
se dobla sin romper

las palabras − flechas;
los poetas − arqueros
y presa a la vez

hoja en blanco −
el universo antes del *Big Bang*
del poema-creación

10 de marzo de 2013

alma primaveral −
mariposa monarca entre
flores y fronteras

golondrinas en
vuelo al Norte soñando
la nueva Luna

narcisos − solecitos
anunciando en jardines
la primavera

tonalli − el Sol
que es nuestra luz interior −
nuestra alma

en algún lugar
hay una quinceañera
en plena flor

plantando semillas
de esperanza en el mundo
en primavera

3 de abril de 2013

in absolute calm
poets carry deep inside
a hurricane

standing alone
a palm tree in a hurricane
bends without breaking

words − arrows;
poets − archers
and prey at once

blank page − the universe
before the Big Bang
of the poem-creation

March 10, 2013

springtime soul −
monarch butterfly between
flowers and borders

swallows in flight
heading North dreaming
the new Moon

daffodils − little suns
announcing in gardens
the arrival of Spring

tonalli − the Sun
that is our inner light −
our soul

somewhere
there is a *quinceañera*
in full bloom

sowing seeds of hope
together for the whole world
this Springtime

April 3, 2013

fuerza de 11 millones –   11 million strong –
tiernas hojas sin fin   boundless tender leaves
de primavera   sprouting in Spring

10 de abril de 2013   *April 10, 2013*

oh la Tierra es   o the Earth is
solo un grano de arena   but a grain of sand
en el universo   in the universe

16 de abril de 2013   *April 16, 2013*

la Tierra – gran jitomate   the Earth – a big round
que precisa de mucho   hearty tomato needing
cuidado y amor   lots of care and love

Día de la Tierra   *Earth Day*
22 de abril de 2012   *April 22, 2013*

para poemas –   for writing poems –
la tinta de lágrimas   the ink of tears
de pena y alegría   of sorrow and joy

no dogmas en poesía –   no dogmas in poetry –
solo amor a la Luna   only love for Moon
Tierra y humanidad   Earth and humankind

upon looking at children of immigrants in Alabama
at the start of a meeting debating on the fate
of Immigration Reform

somos del color   we are brown
de la Madre Tierra –   like Mother Earth –
¡nuestra Tierra Prometida!   our Promised Land!

23 de abril de 2013   *April 23, 2013*

iguanas, ranas
corren por muros
de nuestra casa verde

sintiéndome como
Netzahualcóyotl en
su equipal soñador

un agave azul
es nuestra casita/vida –
¡pátina del corazón!

Padre Viento toca
un canto campanil
este agosto

11 de agosto de 2013

iguanas, frogs
running on walls
of our green home

feeling just like
Netzahualcoyotl on
his dream wicker throne

a blue agave
is our home/life –
patina of our hearts!

Father Wind is
playing a bell song
this August

August 11, 2013

*after an image from the Borbonicus Codex representating poetry
as a Mesoamerican glyph of speech with a blossoming flower*

flor y canto
floreciendo entre tanto
ruido mundanal

5 de noviembre de 2013

flower and song
blossoming in spite of all
the noise in this world

November 5, 2013

letras de un poema –
glifos huecos, sin sentido
sin cómplices

vida en soledad –
el poema sin igual
del universo

8 de noviembre de 2013

letters of a poem –
hollow glyphs, meaningless
without accomplices

life in solitude –
the ultimate poem
of the universe

November 8, 2013

poema – mano abierta
recibiendo y dando luz
al mundo entero

6 de diciembre de 2013

poem – open hand
receiving and giving out
light to the whole world

December 6, 2013

lo que buscas
desde siempre
te está mirando

de un modo todos
nos hallamos de verdad
en otros

1 de enero de 2014

orugas monarcas –
somos capullos, luego
poemas alados

mariposas monarcas –
juntas podemos mover
montañas

5 de enero de 2014

flores, pájaros
en vuelo – todos poemas –
como la Tierra

12 de enero de 2014

dos mariposas
hacen el amor con tanta furia
la tierra tiembla

*tras el temblor de una magnitud
de 6.1 con epicentro en American
Canyon, California
24 de agosto de 2014*

what you seek
has always been
before your eyes

somehow we all
truly find ourselves
in others

January 1, 2014

monarch caterpillars –
we become cocoons, then
winged poems

monarch butterflies –
together we can move
mountains

January 5, 2014

flowers, birds
in full flight – all poems –
like the Earth

January 12, 2014

two butterflies
make love with so much fury
the Earth shakes

*after the 6.1 magnitude earthquake
with an epicenter in American
Canyon, California
August 24, 2014*

Poema	Poem
entro al poema	I enter the poem
igual que a un templo	as I enter a temple
descalzo maravillado	barefoot in awe
dejo todos los artilugios	I leave all gadgets
vestimentas en el portón	garments by the door
al filo del abismo	at the edge of the abyss
me dejo desplomar –	I let myself plunge down –
oh hermanos oh hermanas	o brothers o sisters
el poema me escribe	the poem writes me
24 de febrero de 2014	*February 24, 2014*

Loco

mis puertas
las dejo
sin cerrar

los extraños
me parecen
tan familiares

a todos
los abrazaría
y besaría

cada día
en la calle
hallo a Dios

en vez
de llorar
ahora me río

quiero poner
el mundo
al revés

nada
me convence —
debo de estar loco

3 de agosto de 2009

Crazy

I leave
my doors
unlocked

strangers
look to me
so familiar

I would
embrace and
kiss them all

every day
on the street
I run into God

instead
of crying
now I laugh

I want to
turn the world
upside down

nothing
sways me —
I must be crazy

August 3, 2009

California verde

California verde
verde tierno como
los primeros retoños

tras una semana
de lluvia pertinaz
y unos días de Sol

California verde
una isla, un estado
mental de soñador

oh débiles memorias
un adolescente perenne
en crisis de media vida

California es una larga
autopista a ningún lado
El Camino Real

a la Fiebre del Oro
verde Valle del Silicón
verdes sueños, verdes mentiras

en California los poetas
se hablan verdes solos entre
compradores de comestibles

cerca de los anaqueles
refrigerados de la leche
de soya y el yogurt orgánico –

California verde
verde lechuga
verde aguacate

verde terciopelo de colinas
verde gozo de vacas
verde ensalada de humanidad

California Green

California green
tender green like
first sprouts

after a week
of steady rain
and a few days of Sun

California green
an island, a state
of dreamlike mind

o feeble memories
a perennial teenager
a mid-life crisis

California is a long
freeway to nowhere
El Camino Real

the Gold Rush
green Silicon Valley
green hopes, green lies

in California, poets
talk to themselves – green –
surrounded by food buyers

close to the refrigerated
shelves soy milk
and organic yogurt –

California green
lettus green
avocado green

green velvet hillsides
green delight of cows
green salad of humanity

verde Isla Ángel	green Angel Island
verde alegría, verde desespero	green joy, green despair
verdes cementerios	green cemeteries
verdes campos irrigados	green irrigated fields
oh grandioso apio verde	o grand green celery
California verde	California green
28 de enero de 2012	*January 28, 2012*

Solar Eclipse

I

Mother Moon embraces
Father Sun above the clouds –
we, their children, rejoice!

Mamá Luna abraza
a Papá Sol sobre las nubes –
sus hijos nos regocijamos

Tugann an Mháthair, an Ghealach,
Barróg don Athair, an Ghrian, os cionn na néalta –
Déanaimidne, a gcuid páistí, gairdeas dóibh!

II

the Moon eats the Sun
with kisses and caresses –
they're making celestial love!

la Luna se come
al Sol a besos y caricias –
¡hacen amor celestial!

baineann an Ghealach plaic as an nGrian!
gona bpóga is gona mbarróga –
comhriachtain na spéire!

III

the Moon, the Sun impart
the lesson of Spring –
a wedding ring for all!

la Luna, el Sol dan
la lección primaveral –
¡a todos anillo nupcial!

insíonn an Ghealach is an Ghrian
ceacht earraigh an lae seo –
fáinne pósta do chách!

IV

when the Lady and
Lord of Duality made love –
primordial Big Bang!

la Señora y el Señor
de la Dualidad al amarse –
¡*Big Bang* primordial!

Ometecuhtli = Lord of Duality
Omecihuatl = Lady of Duality
Ometeotl = Deity of Duality

V

Earth, Moon, Sun
Serpent, Quetzal bird, Soul –
a blessing at hand!

*Tlalticpactli, Metztli, Tonatiuh
Coatl, Quetzalli, Tonalli –
nahuatlatolli in matl*

Tierra, Luna, Sol
Serpiente, Quetzal, Tonal –
¡bendición en mano!

an Domhan, an Ghealach, an Ghrian
an Nathair, an Quetzal, an tAnam –
ár mbeannú!

May 27, 2013
Irish (Gaelic) translations by Gabriel Rosenstock

17

América

the accent mark
on top of the letter "é"
in América

is the initial spark
of a firework going up
in the dark night sky

booming loud and bright:
"I'm your country too"
this Fourth of July

July 4th, 2012

América

la tilde de acento
sobre la letra "é"
en América

es la chispa inicial
del cohete pirotécnico
que estalla en la oscuridad

con estrueno y luz:
"yo soy tu nación también
este Cuatro de Julio"

4 de julio de 2012

América

an síneadh fada
ar an litir "é"
in América

an chéad splanc
as tinte ealaíne ag éalú suas
go dtí spéir dhorcha na hoíche

glé os ard an liú:
'Is mise do thírse chomh maith'
an Ceathrú Lá d'Iúil

Irish (Gaelic) translation by Gabriel Rosenstock

América

het accent
op de letter "é"
van de Spaanse benaming
América

is de eerste vonk
van het vuurwerk
dat opstijgt in het donker
van de nachtelijke hemel

knallend luid en hel
"Ik ben ook jouw land"
op deze vierde juli

Dutch translation by Willem M. Roggeman

Yolo Causeway

cruzo
esta carretera puente
para ir a casa

para salir
para tener vida
para ir a ningún lugar

12 de febrero de 2012

Yolo Causeway

I cross
this causeway
to get home

to get away
to get a life
to go nowhere

February 12, 2012

Viajaro especial
y temporal

manejando solo
entre la neblina
el sendero perdí

en algún otro
espacio y tiempo
ahora podría salir

12 de febrero de 2012

Space & Time
Traveller

I lost my way
driving alone
in the tule fog

now I may come
out in some other
space and time

February 12, 2012

Uno con todo

podemos contar los días
del mes mesoamericano con
los dedos de las manos y pies

veinte días, veinte flores
somos calendarios andantes –
uno con todo el alrededor

22 de diciembre de 2012

At One with All

we can count the days
of the Mesoamerican month
with our fingers and toes

twenty days, twenty flowers
we all are walking calendars –
at one with all around us

December 22, 2012

Prometeo poeta

frente
al mundo
estoy inerme

soy ciudad
sin muros
sin guardias

arrasada
por invasores
sin piedad

sólo
me queda
este puñado

de palabras
que cargo
dondequiera

que froto
hasta sacar
este fuego

que comparto
con viajeros
a bordo

del mismo
bote de la vida
a la deriva –

sin tener nada
sino preguntas
sin respuestas

sin importar
esta condena
a cadena perpetua

12 de julio de 2012

Prometheus Poet

I am
disarmed
before the world

I am a city
without walls
without guards

razed
by merciless
invaders

I am left
only with
this fistful

of words
that I carry
everywhere

and rub together
until I draw
this fire

that I share
with travellers
aboard

the same
drifting boat
of life –

having nothing
but questions
without answers

no matter
this life sentence
to perpetual chains

July 12, 2012

Escriba

escribo
con la punta
de la lengua

sobre
aire inasible
siempre fugaz

movido
por la magia
de los signos

escribo
para desandar
lo andado

desatar
estos lazos
que nos atan

los nudos
atorados en
la garganta

escribo
para deshacer
sentencias

romper
los moldes
familiares

abrir
las jaulas
a los canarios

escribo
para dar voz
a los sueños

Scribe

I write
with the tip
of my tongue

over
evanescent
ever fleeting air

moved
by the magic
of signs

I write
to retrace
my steps

to untie
the bonds
that ensnare us

the lumps
knotted up
in our throats

I write
to undo
sentences

to shatter
familiar
molds

to open up
the cages
to the canaries

I write
to give voice
to a thousand-years

milenarios
de la memoria
colectiva

serle fiel
a la Madre Tierra
y sus criaturas

escribo
para no estar
solo al fin

sino contigo
y con todos
luchando

contra
la condena
del olvido

12 de diciembre de 2013

dreams
of collective
memory

to be faithful
to Mother Earth
and its creatures

I write
so as not to be
alone in the end

but with you
and with all
in struggle

against
the curse
of oblivion

December 12, 2013

Fructífero Edén

en el séptimo día
después de crear
la Tierra y el cielo

Dios dijo a las cuatro
direcciones: "ahora
creemos una tierra

como ninguna otra
en todo el mundo
un verdadero Edén

con cauces de agua
rebozantes venidos
de montes nevados

irrigando campos
sin fin con todo tipo
de dulces melones

que la Madre Tierra
dé fruto a las mejores
y más diversas

joyas orgánicas
colgando de árboles
como almendras verdes

duraznos, pistachos
cerezas, aguacates
granadas, limones

dejando en el suelo
corazones sonrientes
jitomates, fresas

que manos humanas
acaricien y empaquen
dones de gran sabor

Fruitful Eden

on the seventh day
after creating the Earth
and the sky

God said to the four
directions, "now
let's create a land

like no other land
in the entire world
a true Eden

with overflowing
waterways coming
from snowy mountains

irrigating endless
fields of every sort
of sweet melons

let Mother Earth
give fruit to the best
and most varied

organic jewels
hanging from trees
as green almonds

peaches, pistachios
cherries, avocados
pomegranates, lemons

leaving on the ground
smiling hearts
tomatoes, strawberries

may human hands
caress and pack
the tastiest of gifts

en las más efectivas
maneras para llegar
frescos y sin mácula

a estantes de verduras
de todos los mercados
de esta gran nación" –

Dios estaba contento
de ver los vastos campos
verdes y así mandó

frescas brisas marinas
sobre colinas tostadas
por el Sol al lado de valles

entonces Dios se zambulló
en el largo acueducto
para después afirmar:

"California es una obra
maestra real gracias a mí
y a manos humanas"

5 de julio de 2013

in the most effective
ways so they arrive
fresh and without blemish

to the produce stands
of every market
of this big nation" –

and God was pleased
to see the vast green
fields and so He sent

cooling sea breezes
over sun-baked hills
bordering valleys

then God took a dip
into the long aqueduct
and afterwards said

"California is a true
masterpiece thanks
to me and human hands"

July 5, 2013

Mariposas sin fronteras	Borderless Butterflies
I	I
o mariposas monarcas – reinas de las mariposas	o monarch butterflies – queens of the butterflies
todas pasan por cuatro etapas en su propia vida:	you all go through four stages in your own life:
huevito, oruga crisálida y mariposa desarrollada –	little egg, caterpillar chrysalis and then fully-grown butterfly –
primero salen de huevitos como orugas bebés	first you come out from little eggs as baby caterpillars
en seguida se pasan dos semanas comiendo de un algodoncillo	next you spend two weeks feeding on a milkweed plant
hasta convertirse en orugas adultas desarrolladas	until becoming fully-grown caterpillars –
y se adherirán a una rama o una hoja	you will attach yourselves to a stem or a leaf
usando seda se convertirán en crisálidas	and using silk you will turn into chrysalises
para así empezar el proceso mágico de la metamorfosis	and thus begin the magic process of metamorphosis

tras diez días	after ten days
de los capullos	you will emerge
emergerán	from the pupas
como bellas	as beautiful
mariposas monarcas	monarch butterflies
para luego volar	and fly away

II	II
en febrero o marzo	in February and March
las mariposas de	the butterflies of the first
la primera generación	generation come out
salen de hibernación	from hibernation
para copular	to find mates
y migrar al norte	and migrate north
en marzo y abril	in March and April
ponen huevos	they lay eggs
en algodoncillos	on milkweed plants
y mueren después	and die after a short
de una corta vida de	life span of only
solo dos a seis semanas	two to six weeks
la siguiente generación	the next generation
pasa por las mismas	goes again through
cuatro etapas de vida –	the four life stages –
los algodoncillos	milkweed plants
proveen a las mariposas	provide butterflies
con protección	with protection
sus hojas tienen	their leaves have
substancias tóxicas	substances toxic
para los pájaros	to most birds

III	III
la segunda generación	the second generation
de mariposas monarcas	of monarch butterflies
nace en mayo y junio	is born in May and June

y luego la tercera
generación nace
en julio y agosto

ambas generaciones
pasan por las mismas
etapas de vida

como la primera
generación de mariposas
pasó en vida

IV

la cuarta generación
tiene un destino distinto
de las otras tres

la cuarta generación
nace en septiembre
y octubre

pasa por las cuatro
etapas de vida de
las otras generaciones

pero la cuarta generación
de mariposas monarcas
no muere tras una breve vida

de solo dos a seis semanas –
por su parte esta generación
de mariposas monarcas

migra a climas más
calurosos como México
y California

y vivirá más tiempo
de seis a ocho meses
para poder completar

and then the third
generation is born
in July and August

both generations
go through the exactly
the same life cycle

as the first generation
of monarch butterflies
went through in life

IV

the fourth generation
has a different fate
from the other three

the fourth generation
is born in September
and October

it goes through the four
stages of the life cycle
of the other generations

but the fourth generation
of monarch butterflies
doesn't die after a short life

of only two to six weeks –
instead this generation
of monarch butterflies

migrate to warmer
climates like Mexico
and California

and will live longer
for six to eight months
to be able to complete

la larga migración
y comenzar otra vez
el maravilloso ciclo de vida

de las mariposas monarcas –
las más singulares criaturas
migrantes sin fronteras

22 de agosto 2014

its long migration
and start over again
the marvelous life cycle

of the monarch butterflies –
the ultimate borderless
migrant creatures!

August 22, 2014

Para los Nueve del Capitolio   For the Capitol Nine

para los nueve estudiantes arrestados
en el Capitolio Estatal de Arizona
por protestar la ley SB 1070
el 20 de abril de 2010

to the nine students arrested
at the Arizona State Capitol
protesting SB 1070
on April 20, 2010

carnalitos
y carnalitas
hermanos
y hermanas:

carnalitos
y carnalitos
brothers
and sisters:

desde lejos
podemos oír
sus corazones latir

from afar
we can hear
your heart beats

ellos son
los tambores
de la Tierra

they are
the drums
of the Earth

nuestra gente
les sigue de cerca
sus pasos

our people
follow closely
your steps

como guerreros
de la justicia
y la paz

as warriors
of justice
and peace

enfrentan
la Bestia
del odio

you take on
the Beast
of hatred

el uso
discriminatorio
de la policía

the unlawful
police enforcement
of discrimination

se encadenan
a las puertas del
Capitolio Estatal

you chain yourselves
to the doors of
the State Capitol

para que el terror
no se escape hacia
nuestras calles

so that terror
will not leak out
to our streets

sus voces	your voices
sus acciones	your actions
su valentía	your courage
no nos las pueden	can't be taken
ya arrebatar	away from us
ni encarcelar	and put in jail
ustedes son nueve	you are nine
jóvenes guerreros	young warriors
como nueve luceros	like nine sky stars
son la esperanza	you are the hope
los mejores sueños	the best dreams
de nuestra nación	of our nation
sus rostros	your faces
son radiantes	are radiant
como el Sol	as the Sun
y romperán	they will break
esta negra noche	this dark night
para un nuevo día	for a new day
sí, *carnalitas*	yes, *carnalitas*
y *carnalitos*	and *carnalitos:*
todos nuestros	all our sisters
hermanas y hermanos	all our brothers
no necesitan papeles	need no papers
para probar	to prove once
de una vez	and for all
"somos humanos	"we are humans
como ustedes son –	just like you are –
no somos criminales"	we are not criminals"
nuestra petición es:	our plea comes to
"¡NO a la criminalización!	"NO to criminalization!
¡SÍ a la legalización!"	YES to legalization!"
20 de abril de 2010	*Abril 20, 2014*

Soñadores

somos todos
soñadores
– *dreamers* –

juntos
subimos
montañas

nada
nos puede
ahora detener –

como
mariposas
monarcas

cruzamos
fronteras
prejuicios –

el poder
de la luz
de la vida

el compromiso
de uno con
el otro

esta devoción
sin límites
nos guían

todos somos
soñadores
– *dreamers* –

7 de septiembre de 2012

Dreamers

we are all
dreamers
– *soñadores* –

together
we climb
mountains

nothing
can now
stop us –

just like
monarch
butterflies

we cross
borders
prejudices –

the power
of light
of life

the commitment
of one
to another

this boundless
devotion –
guide us

we all are
dreamers
– *soñadores* –

September 7, 2012

Living Targets

given away
by the dark tone
of our skin

the flapping
colorful birds
in our tongue

we are here
walking suspects
living targets –

always free
as breathing air
in the loving arms

of each other

July 15, 2013

Self-Questions
For Possible Suspects*

do you prefer
tacos al pastor
to hot dogs

crave messy
enchiladas
to burgers

still pray
in Spanish
and say

"¡ay, caramba!"
when you are
really surprised

can only hum
"The Star-Spangled
Banner"

every time
the national anthem
is played in public

wear airy
guayaberas
outdoors in the heat

have a permanent
deep tan without
any sunbathing –

be aware you
may be under
reasonable suspicion

no matter
if your are a native
born citizen

whose ancestors
were in Arizona
long before

the United States
moved the border
southward

June 30, 2012

*With reasonable suspicion under Section 2(B) –
racial profiling due to Arizona SB 1070

Saguaros

en Mesa, Arizona
los saguaros apuntando

al cielo del desierto
le dicen a todos:

"abran los brazos,
extiendan las manos;

no se vuelvan duros
puños sin corazón"

8 de noviembre de 2011

Saguaros

in Mesa, Arizona
saguaros pointing

to the desert sky
tell all around:

"open your arms,
extend your hands

don't become hard
heartless fists"

November 8, 2011

Convicciones

digo patria
raza, fe

sombras
a mi lado

se tragan
todo esto –

ahora
me quedo

con pocas
palabras

más voluntad
alma, corazón

15 de diciembre de 2012

Convictions

I say country
kin, faith

shadows
besides me

swallow
everything –

now
I am left

with few
words

more will
soul, heart

December 15, 2012

El tiempo ha llegado

el tiempo ha llegado
para reclamarnos
unos a los otros

para demandar
al Faraón: "deja a nuestro
pueblo vivir en paz"

7 de febrero de 2013

Time Has Come

time has come
to reclaim ourselves
and each other

to demand Pharaoh:
"let our people
live in peace"

February 7, 2013

Dialéctica de Moisés

un continuo *"no"* –
el mundo es un muro
alto, mudo, cruel

un cambio a *"sí"* –
el Mar Rojo se abre
a la Tierra Prometida

12 diciembre de 2013

Moses Dialectics

a persistent *"no"* –
the world is a tall
mute, cruel wall

a change to *"yes"* –
the Red Sea opens up
to the Promised Land

December 12, 2013

Puerta del tiempo

esta puerta abres
como niño un día
en la mañana

para cerrarla
luego lleno de canas
a medianoche

6 de marzo de 2012

Time's Door

you open this door
as a kid one day
in the morning

and end up closing it
now full of gray hair
at midnight

March 6, 2012

Noche y día

hasta en la noche
invernal más oscura
desolada y fría

llevo por dentro
un veraniego día
lleno de Sol

22 de diciembre de 2013

Night & Day

even in the darkest
coldest, most desolate
midwinter night

I carry within me
a Summer day
full of sunlight

December 22, 2013

Plegaria

en el Solsticio Invernal de 2011
en preparación para el Sol Flor

en la más larga
la más oscura noche
de todo el año

invoco la luz
de los sabios ancestros
a mi corazón

la flor, el canto
el precioso plumaje
de sus memorias

el Aire, el Fuego
el Agua, la Tierra son
ahora familia mía

ahora soy árbol
soy nube, soy serpiente
soy jade, soy ave

soy de aquí, de allá
soy de dondequiera
de ningún lado

el Sol es mi padre
la Luna es mi madre –
todos somos hermanos

todas somos hermanas –
in lak' ech – "tú eres
mi otro yo"

llevo en el pecho
un *tonalli*, un aliento
una huella del Sol –

una flor del mil
petálos me está abriendo
¡ay! el corazón

21 de diciembre de 2011

Prayer

on the 2011 Winter Solstice
getting ready for the Flower Sun

on the longest
the darkest night
of the whole year

I call forth the light
of the wise ancestors
to my heart

the flower, the song
the precious feathers
of their memories

Wind, Fire
Water, Earth are
now forever my family

now I am tree
I am cloud, I am serpent
I am jade, I am bird

I am from here, from there
from everywhere
and nowhere

the Sun is my father
the Moon is my mother –
we all are brothers

we all are sisters –
in lak' ech – "you are
my other I"

within my chest
I carry a *tonalli*, a breath
a trace of the Sun –

a flower of a thousand
petals is opening
o my heart!

December 21, 2011

En poesía

en poesía
estás solo
como poeta

eres un árbol
parado alto
en la noche

recuerdas
las melodías
de tu madre

los cuentos
y risotadas
de tu padre

las burlas
de hermanos
y hermanas

los susurros
al oído de amigos
y amantes

en poesía
estás solo
en compañía

de la Luna
las nubes
estrellas

con el primer
y último poeta
de la Tierra

en poesía
hoy, ayer
y mañana

In Poetry

in poetry
you are alone
as poet

a lone tree
standing tall
in the night

you remember
your mother's
melodies

your father's
tall stories
and loud laughter

your brothers'
and sisters'
taunts and cheers

the whispers
of friends and lovers
in your ears –

in poetry
you are alone
in company

of the Moon
the clouds
the stars

with the first
and last poet
of this Earth

in poetry
today, yesterday
and tomorrow

se vuelven
todos uno
otra vez

en poesía
nunca estás
de veras solo

25 de agosto de 2014

become
all just one
once again

in poetry
you are never
truly alone

August 25, 2014

II Fuego / Fire

batiendo oscuras	striking dark
piedras-palabras poetas	word-stones poets
dan fuego-poesía	draw fire-poetry

Del corazón

poesía – el silencio –
la flor del corazón
de las palabras

4 de julio de 2011

*a la memoria de Adrienne Rich
(1929-2012)*

el día de tu partida
lluvia pero siempre
vivas tu risa y luz

28 de marzo de 2012

nopal en flor
corazón en tu cocina –
llamado a la acción

19 de abril de 2012

mi madre me enseñó
a dar la mano como ángel
sin mirar a quién

mi madre entra
como luz por mi ventana
el Día de las Madres

12 de mayo de 2012

silencio – agujero negro
sorbiendo estrellas y luz
al centro de galaxias

19 de septiembre de 2012

From the Heart

poetry – the silence –
the flower in full bloom
in the heart of words

July 4, 2011

*in memory of Adrienne Rich
(1929-2012)*

the day of your passing
it rained but forever alive
your laughter and light

March 28, 2012

cactus in bloom
a heart in your kitchen –
a call for action

April 19, 2012

my mother taught me
to offer my hand like angel
without regard to whom

my mother comes in
like sunlight through my window
on Mother's Day

May 12, 2012

silence – black hole
sucking up stars and light
at the galaxies' core

September 19, 2012

una escalera	just a ladder
para trepar el muro	to climb the border wall
a tu corazón	to reach your heart
y divisar contigo	and with you search for
horizonte y estrellas	the horizon and the stars

2 de julio de 2013   *July 2, 2013*

aquí y ahora –	here and now –
no sólo tú y yo, sino todos	not just you and me, but all
en pleno vuelo	of us, in full flight

9 de junio de 2012   *June 9, 2012*

un beso es un beso	a kiss is a kiss
un abrazo es un abrazo	an embrace is an embrace
amor es siempre amor –	love is always love –
todos somos iguales bajo	we are all equal under
un mismo sol y arco iris	the same Sun and rainbow

26 de junio de 2013   *June 26, 2013*

"We'll make the border with Mexico
look like 'the Berlin Wall'"
– Senator John McCain

"Haremos que la frontera con México
parezca como 'el Muro de Berlín'"
– Senador John McCain

mariposas monarcas	monarch butterflies
seguirán sobrevolando	will keep on flying over
el nuevo "Muro de Berlín" –	this new "Berlin Wall" –
no "drones", no guardias, no torres	no drones, no guards, no towers
pararán deseos alados	to stop winged aspirations

28 de junio de 2013   *June 28, 2013*

tus huesos junto
Federico, bajo la luz
de la Luna, de toda
la vida enamorado
como el Sol andaluz

El Salvador
muy hondo lo llevo
como el corazón
de Monseñor Romero
floreciendo en catedral

no hay palabras
para este poema – solo
silencio amoroso

8 de noviembre de 2013

deambulando
oh más solo en multitud
que en soledad

24 de noviembre de 2013

las llaves forman
las letras de poemas
para abrir corazones

28 de noviembre de 2013

escribo versos
que solo tus ojos
pueden decifrar

29 de noviembre de 2013

I am gathering
your bones, Federico
under the Moonlight
in love with all of life
like the Andalusian Sun

I carry El Salvador
very deeply within me
as the heart of Monsignor
Romero flowering
under the cathedral

no words
for this poem – only
loving silence

November 8, 2013

wandering around
o more alone in a crowd
than in solitude

November 24, 2013

iron keys arrange
themselves as letters
of poems to open hearts

November 28, 2013

I write verses
that only your eyes
can decipher

November 29, 2013

Chichen Itzá –
corazón de piedra mágico
brillando noche y día

9 de diciembre de 2013

oh un poema abraza
besa el punto fugaz
llamado presente

17 de diciembre de 2013

Sol, todos traemos
en alma y corazón
tu fuego, tu luz

21 de diciembre de 2013

atrás de mi casa
dos ardillas hacen vida
no importa el frío invernal

jovial colibrí –
sonrisa voladora
besando flores

que estrellas claras
siempre iluminen
tu cielo nocturno

23 de diciembre de 2013

en algún lugar
otros ojos admiran
el universo

Chichen Itzá –
enchanted stone heart
glowing night and day

December 9, 2013

o a poem embraces
kisses the fleeting point
called present time

December 17, 2013

Sun, we all carry
in our soul, our heart
your fire, your light

December 15, 2013

in my backyard
two squirrels go on with life
no matter the Winter cold

joyous hummingbird –
fluttering smile
kissing flowers

may bright stars
always illuminate
your night sky

December 23, 2013

somewhere
other eyes stare in awe
at the universe

quemo mis naves –
ahora sin retorno estoy
todo en tus manos

oh escuchemos
las flamas del corazón
aún por decifrar

12 de enero de 2014

quetzal en vuelo –
nuestro floricanto siempre
libre en el cielo

4 de julio de 2014

I burn my ships
with no way back now –
I am all in your hands

o let us listen to
yet to be deciphered
flames of our hearts

January 12, 2014

quetzal bird in flight –
our flower song always
boundless in the sky

July 4, 2014

Plegaria de amor

que el amor
nos sorprenda
sin previo aviso

que el amor
venga a nosotros
como dulce aire

que el amor
nos mueva a amar
a otros así

veloz como
estrella fugaz
en la oscuridad

oliendo
el cabello sedoso
de nuestro amor

como nos amamos
a nosotros mismos
y a los que nos aman

recordándonos
que nunca jamás
estamos solos

encendiendo
las brasas de
su viejo fulgor

tomando acciones
por los más pobres
los más necesitados

aun cuando
estamos solos
sintiéndonos solos

llenándonos
la vida con calor
luz y alegría

concediéndonos
aún más amor
sobreacogedor

5 de febrero de 2012

Love Prayer

may love
surprise us
unexpectedly

swiftly like
a shooting star
in the night sky

reminding us
we are never
ever alone

even when
we are alone
feeling lonesome

may love
come to us
as sweet air

smelling
our beloved's
silky hair

igniting
the embers
of a long fire

filling life
with warmth
joy and light

may love
move us
to love others

as we love
ourselves and
those who love us

taking actions
for the poorest
the neediest

rewarding us
with even more
overflowing love

February 5, 2012

Poeta a los seis años

I

tengo seis años
y estoy en casa
de mi abuela Chayo

en Wilmington,
California, mis padres
están en su labor

mi abuela Chayo
es delgada y pálida como
el interior de una pera

"ve y lávate
esas manos sucias"
me dice

yo me las lavo
tan bien y limpias
como puedo

pero ella sigue
diciéndome algo
acerca de mis manos...

tras yo lavármelas
con jabón en polvo
y agua caliente

dos, tres veces,
mis manos ahorita
relucen de coloradas

"ve y vuélvete a lavar
esas cochinas manos…"
la oigo decir

Poet at Six Years Old

I

I'm six years old
at Grandma
Chayo's home

in Wilmington,
California, my parents
are at work

Grandma Chayo
is thin and pale
the flesh of a pear

"go and wash
those dirty hands"
she tells me

I wash them
as good and
clean as I can

but she keeps
saying something
about my hands...

after I wash them
with powder soap
and hot water

two, three times,
now my hands
are glowing red

"go and wash again
those dirty hands…"
I hear her saying

II

Carlos, mi hermano
menor con pelo medio
rubio y de piel güero

ya está sentado
sorbiendo sopa
con un cucharón

oh Madre dónde
andas para salvarme
de tu propia Madre

a los seis años
siento mi destino
sellado para siempre

soy un patito prieto
feo que nadie jamás
se atreverá a amar

III

a los seis años todavía
pero ahora estoy en
Guadalajara, México

yendo a visitar
a mi abuelita Elvira
por primera vez

la hallo sentada
en un equipal
bajo el Sol

cepillándose
su larga cabellera
que tocaba el piso

II

Carlos, my younger
brother with blondish
hair and White skin

is already seated
slurping his soup
with a big spoon

o Mother where
are you to save me
from your own Mother

at six year old
I feel my fate
sealed forever

I am a dark ugly
duckling nobody
would ever dare love

III

still six years old
but I am now in
Guadalajara, Mexico

going to visit
mi abuelita Elvira
for the first time

I find her seated
in a wicker chair
out in the Sun

brushing her long
hair touching
the floor

ella es redondita
prieta y dulce
como una ciruela

me abraza fuerte
entre sus brazos
"*m'ijo,* te esperaba

a ti por tanto tiempo;
eres mi bendición" –
yo me siento gema

sin saberlo
ahora así sé:
el amor me salva

26 de septiembre de 2012

she is round
dark and sweet
as a fresh plum

she holds me
tight in her arms
"*m'ijo,* I was waiting

for you for so long;
you're my blessing" –
I feel like a gemstone

somehow
I now know
love saves me

September 26, 2012

Abuelita Elvira – Luna llena mía

I

tenía yo seis años
cuando te conocí
Abuelita Elvira

yo, un *pochito* del
Norte en busca de
sus raíces tormentosas

Papá, salvándonos
al llevar a su familia al Sur
a México lleno de Sol

y tú, una Luna llena
brillando en el cielo
oscuro de mi niñez

oh Gran Madre de
susurros y suspiros
venciendo las noches

hasta los helechos
se inclinaban ante
tu poder, tu esplendor

contigo aprendí
el alfabeto mágico
de hechizos y plegarias

el poder curativo
de plantas, remedios
para cuerpo y alma

II

tu maravillosa casona
era como el laberinto
de Minotauro en Creta

Grandma Elvira – My Own Full Moon

I

I was six years old
when I met you
Grandma Elvira

I, a *pochito*, from
the North looking for
his stormy roots

Papá, saving us
by taking his family
South to sunny Mexico

and you, a full Moon
shining in the dark sky
of my childhood

o Great Mother
of whispers and sighs
overcoming nights

even ferns would bow
to your mighty power
and amazing splendor

with you, I learned
the magic alphabet
of spells and prayers

the healing power
of plants, remedies
for the body and soul

II

your amazing big house
was like the Labyrinth
of Minotaur in Crete

abrir el gran portón
de tu casona era traspasar
un mágico portal

una selva crecía
en tu patio central
junto al pozo a China

oh Abuelita Elvira
me tomabas de la mano
junto a la tuya cada vez

que me bendecías
me santiguabas y
me besabas en la frente

III

pero hiciste el error
de darle tu casona
en testamento en vida

a tu hijo, mi padre
quien en naipes perdió
nuestra casa y la tuya

yo me tuve que ir
al Norte solo en busca
de un nuevo inicio

dieciocho años tenía
cuando en Los Ángeles
me dieron aviso

que tú, Abuela, habías
muerto sin casa, desolada
en Guadalajara, México

tu destino fue el de una
verdadera *Cihuacóatl*
la Mujer Serpiente

opening the board wooden
door of your big home was
to go through a magic portal

a jungle grew
in your central patio
next to the well to China

o Grandma Elvira
you held my hand
in yours every time

you blessed me, made
a sign of the cross, and
kissed me on the forehead

III

you made the error
of willing your big home
while still alive

to your son, my father
who lost our home
And yours playing cards

I had to go North
alone in seach of
a new beginning

eighteen years old
I was in Los Angeles
when I was advised

you, Grandma, had died
homeless, heart-broken
in Guadalajara, Mexico

you met the fate
of a true *Cihuacoatl*
the Snake Woman

tu tierra, tu vida
te las arrebataron
la perfidia, la maldad

tu nagual volador
tu sabio tecolote batido
en pleno vuelo sin piedad

tú, *Llorona* curandera
me llamas sin tregua
desde el Arroyo del Olvido

IV

oigo, Abuela, tu llanto
junto con tu canto
dándome vida otra vez

y cuando te veo
en la pantalla de cine
encarnada como *Última*

en la película *Bendíceme,
Última* basada en la novela
de Rudolfo Anaya

te siento junto mí
bendiciéndome a través
de las barreras del tiempo

dándome tus bendiciones
de bondad, compasión
tolerancia, belleza…

oh Abuelita Elvira
Luna llena de plenitud
en el oscuro cielo mío

22 de febrero de 2013

your land, your life
taken away from you
by perfidy, by evil

your flying *nagual*
a wise owl struck down
without pity in full flight

you, a healing *Llorona*
call to me without rest
from Oblivion Creek

IV

Abuela, I hear your weeping
mingled with your songs
giving me life once again

and when I see you
on the theater screen
as *Ultima* incarnate

in the movie *Bless Me,
Última* based on the novel
by Rudolfo Anaya

I feel you next to me
blessing me across
all barriers of time

giving me your blessings
of kindness, compassion
tolerance, beauty…

o Grandma Elvira
bountiful full Moon
in my dark sky forever

February 22, 2013

Suchitoto / Pájaro Flor / Flower Bird

pueblo mágico
donde el duro corazón
se hace un pájaro flor

magical town
where the hardest heart
turns into a flower bird

"Suchitoto" en
náhuatl – *Xóchitl* (Flor)
y *Tótotl* (Pájaro)

"Suchitoto" in
Nahuatl – *Xochitl* (Flower)
and *Tototl* (Bird)

la gente aquí
puede dar vida a pájaros
con pétalos de flor

the folks here
can give life to birds
with flower petals

las flores aquí
son pájaros que cantan
llenos de color

the flowers here
are singing birds
full of color

Museo Alejandro Coto, Suchitoto, El Salvador

tras este portón
ventanales con rejas
hay un laberinto
donde la historia patria
corre veloz como niño

behind this broad door
big iron-grated windows
there is a labyrinth
where this country's history
runs as fast as a youngster

espejo del cielo
oh fuente de la eterna
juventud, te ríes
como la sabia monja
Sor Juana Inés de la Cruz

mirror of the sky
o fountain of eternal
youth, you laugh
like the wise nun
Sor Juana Inés de la Cruz

por escaleras
de piedra el pasado
baja a soñar

down stairs of stone
the past descends
to dream

piedra estrella luz
de los cuatro vientos
guía del corazón

stone star light
of the four winds
guide of our heart

oh flor de piedra
Venus matinal, pájaro
presto a volar

nada es real – todo es
una fuente, un sueño
como la vida

la Luna aquí
es una flor que canta
como pájaro

en El Salvador
la Luna llena es una
pupusa celestial

16 de noviembe de 2013

o flower of stone
morning Venus, bird
ready to take flight

nothing's real – everything's
a fountain, a dream
just like life

the Moon here
is a flower singing
like a sky bird

in El Salvador
the full Moon is one
celestial *pupusa*

November 16, 2013

Los volcanes aquí toman la palabra

*a los miles de indígenas pipiles y ladinos masacrados
impunemente tras la insurrección de 1932 en El Salvador*

los volcanes aquí
toman de los pájaros
la palabra

ante el silencio
el dolor de los pueblos
ancestrales

desolados
cerca de las faldas
del volcán Izalco

heridas vivas
aún sin cicatrizar
a flor de tierra

fosas colectivas
abiertas al cielo
en el olvido –

el pasado
toma al amanecer
la palabra
**

los volcanes aquí
toman de truenos
la palabra

oh dios *Tláloc*
Señor de las Tormentas
ahora lamenta

las ráfagas
de ametralladoras
y fusiles

aún resonando
en la distancia
en la memoria

por los campos
las plazas, las fincas
los caminos –

los maizales
los cafetales toman
la palabra
***

los volcanes aquí
toman de las nubes
la palabra

oh campesinos
de sombrero de palma
de *Cuzcatlán*

como aves en vuelo
caen con el pecho
ensangrentado

cristos de manta
traspasados por balas
ciegas sin piedad

padres e hijos
vecinos victimados
sin distinción –

las familias
recordando toman
la palabra
****

los volcanes aquí
toman del mar
la palabra

las piedras negras
antes lava ahora
suave arena hablan

las olas son
lenguas testimoniando
sin parar

las masacres
de miles de pipiles
y ladinos –

los volcanes aquí
toman de los muertos
ahora la palabra

invocándolos
a los cuatro vientos
para nunca olvidar

17 de noviembre de 2012

Volcanoes Here Speak

*to the thousands of indigenous Pipil peoples and Mestizos
massacred with impunity after the insurrection of 1932 in El Salvador*

volcanoes here
take on the language
of birds to speak

about
the silent grief
of ancestral towns

now forsaken
all around Izalco
the volcano

open wounds
of the Earth
in need of healing

collective graves
facing the sky
in oblivion –

the past
at day's break
starts to speak up

**
volcanoes here
learn from thunders
to speak

o, god *Tláloc*
Lord of the Storms
now laments

the mortal sounds
of machine guns
and rifles

still reverberating
in the distance
in the memory

alongside fields
town squares, farms
countryside roads –

corn fields
coffee growing grounds
do speak up

***
volcanoes here
inspired by clouds
start to speak

o, peasants
of *Cuzcatlán*
wearing palm hats

as birds in flight
you go down with
breasts bleeding

white cotton Christs
riddled by blind
merciless bullets

fathers and sons
neighbors victimized
without distinction –

families begin
speaking up
by remembering

****
volcanoes here
speak up loudly
as the sea

black stones
once lava now soft
sand speak

sea waves
are tongues giving
nonstop testimony

the massacres
of thousands of Indians
and Mestizos –

volcanoes here
now speak
for the dead

invoking them
to the four winds
so to never forget

November 17, 2012

Dolor

mi dolor
lo llevo
dentro

ciego
sordo
mudo

mi dolor
no tiene
nombre

inicio
cura
ni fin –

mi dolor
lo llevo
solo

hasta
hallar
tu dolor

entonces
nuestro
mutuo dolor

compartimos
como pan
de cada día

26 de enero de 2010

Grief

I carry
this grief
within me

I carry
my grief
alone

blind
deaf
mute

until
I find
your grief

my grief
has no
name

then
our mutual
grief

start
cure
nor end −

we share
as our daily
bread

January 26, 2010

Canto cardenche / Cactus Song!

"To sing canción cardenche, you must feel it –
it penetrates like the thorns of the cardenche fruit,
which are even more painful when they are pulled out."
– Guadalupe Salazar Vásquez, singer

canto cardenche –
hieres hondo el corazón
¡oh sangre en flor!

como espina
como lengua de fuego
como pena de amor

el viento vuelto
canto, lamento, llanto –
cardenche en flor

8 de diciembre de 2013

cactus song –
you deeply wound the heart
o blood in bloom!

like a thorn
like a tongue of fire
like grief-stricken love

the wind became
song, lament, weeping –
a cactus in bloom

December 8, 2013

Bendiciones de amor

mi abuelita
y mi abuelito
me bendijeron

Mamá y Papá
me dieron también
su bendición

santiguándome
besándome
en la frente –

oh cada vez
que me besan
en la frente

me siento bendecido –
todo amor siempre es
¡una bendición real!

24 de enero de 2013

Love Blessing

my grandma
and my grandpa
blessed me

Mamá and *Papá*
also gave me
their benediction

blessing me
kissing me
on my forehead –

o every time
I am kissed
on my forehead

I feel so blessed! –
all love always is
a true blessing!

January 24, 2013

Duende

*a Nino de los Reyes**

el duende
es un ángel
caído del cielo

con las alas
derretidas
por el Sol

bendecido
por la Tierra
y la Luna

que pone
de cabeza
al mundo

el duende
es la rama
en llamas

que arrasa
imparable
los trigales

es el filo
del cuchillo
del canto

que nos clava
y desclava
el corazón

el duende
es el Cristo
que se baja

de su cruz
y se pone
a zapatear

se despoja
de su corona
de espinas

y cantando
se nos muere
en los brazos

y resucita
al tercer día
de su muerte

el duende
es la rosa
en la boca

que nos sangra
y nos viste
¡ay! de negro

el alma para
hacerla antorcha
en la oscuridad

14 de abril de 2014

Nino de los Reyes, conocido como "El Toro del Flamenco", interpretó bailando flamenco el papel de Federico García Lorca en la puesta en escena de "Blood Wedding/Bodas de sangre" de Federico García Lorca en una nueva versión en inglés de Caridad Svich y dirigida por Anton Juan en la Universidad de Notre Dame.

Duende

*to Nino de los Reyes**

duende is
an angel fallen
from heaven

with wings
wholly melted
by the Sun

but blessed
by the Earth
and the Moon

able to turn
the world
on its head

duende
is a branch
in flames

scorching
irrepressibly
the wheat fields

it is the sharp
edge of the knife
of the song

that nails
and unnails
our heart

duende is
the Christ
who comes down

from his cross
to rhythmically
stamp his feet

takes off
his crown
of thorns

and dies
singing in
our arms

and comes
back to life
on the third day

duende is
that rose
on our mouth

that makes us
bleed and dresses
our soul

o in black
making it a torch
in the darkness

Abril 14, 2014

Nino de los Reyes, known as "El Toro del Flamenco," played the role of Federico García Lorca dancing flamenco in the production of "Blood Wedding" by Federico García Lorca in a new English version by Caridad Svich and directed by Anton Juan at University of Notre Dame.

Federico García Lorca / Roque Dalton / Gloria Anzaldúa

oh poetas del mundo	o poets of the world
de ayer, mañana, siempre	from yesterday, tomorrow
sin fronteras	forever borderless
hermano del alma	soulmate brother
hermano en lucha	brother in struggle
hermana mestiza	Mestiza sister
pusieron en riesgo	you risked your lives
sus vidas en versos – y ante	in poems – choosing
mentiras, la verdad	truth over lies
9 de diciembre de 2013	*December 9, 2013*

III Agua / Water

gotas en nubes
de la mano se dejan
caer como lluvia

droplets in clouds
join hands and let go
falling as rain

De lluvia, ríos, mar

en primavera
llueve el cielo llorando –
narcisos sonríen

21 de marzo de 2011

jitomates rojos –
corazones locos
del verano

chiles verdes
alegres cuelgan de matas
como sonrisas

las calabacitas
salen como de acuerdo
a mitad del jardín

los elotes crecen
como tamalitos de hoja –
ofrendas al Sol

los duraznos son
nalguitas de ángeles
orando en ramas

en un arbusto
granadas coloradas
comienzan a reír

serpientes vivas
se yerguen con cuidado
tiempo, agua, luz

17 de agosto de 2011

From Rain, Rivers, Sea

in Spring
the sky weeps rain –
daffodils smile

March 21, 2011

ripe tomatoes –
crazy hearts
of mid-Summer

green chiles hang
happily from bushes
like lush smiles

zucchini squashes
appear as if by agreement
in the middle of the garden

ears of corn grow
like husk wrapped *tamalitos* –
offerings to the Sun

peaches are
the little butts of angels
praying on branches

in a small tree
red pomegranates
begin to laugh

serpents spring to life
with care, time
water, light

August 17, 2011

"Yo tengo un sueño..."
– Martin Luther King, Jr.

toda la humanidad
yendo libre, sin obstáculos
como ríos al mar

16 de enero 2012

la media Luna –
tajada de jícama
en el cielo-mar

el cielo al alba –
límpida laguna azul
tras la tempestad

14 de abril de 2012

todos somos uno –
anunciamos la lluvia
como arco iris

31 de mayo de 2012

Monte Albán –
mística flor de piedra
coronando el monte

Monte Albán, Oaxaca
19 de agosto de 2012

Mitla – un sueño
en tableros de piedra
en pleno vuelo

tumba de Mitla –
cruz enterrada viva
en carne honda

"I have a dream..."
– Martin Luther King, Jr.

all humanity
running free, unimpeded
like rivers to the sea

January 16, 2012

the half Moon –
a slice of jicama
in the sky-sea

the sky at dawn –
a limpid blue lagoon
after the storm

April 14, 2012

we all are one –
we announce the coming rain
like a rainbow

May 31, 2012

Monte Albán –
mystic flower of stone
crowing the mountain

Monte Albán, Oaxaca
August 12, 2012

Mitla – a dream
in stone panels
in full flight

Mitla tomb –
cross buried alive
in deep flesh

las cuatro cúpulas
del templo de San Pablo
son chupacabras

Mitla, Oaxaca
21 de agosto de 2012

tortugas de mar –
poetas poniendo huevos
poemas en la playa

oh cuántas criaturas
de estos huevos-poemas
no serán tortugas

Mazunte, Oaxaca
3 de septiembre de 2012

oh Luna llena
posas tus pies de luz
entre las plantas
de tomates del jardín –
bolas de sangre y plata

oh luna llena
gran bandeja plateada
promesa del cielo
sueño de un niñito –
conejito celestial

23 de junio de 2013

dulce sonrisa de Sol
cada tajada
de melón

tu guiño de Sol –
oh girasol dando luz
al campo al mediodía

the four domes
of the temple of San Pablo
are *chupacabras*

Mitla, Oaxaca
August 21, 2012

sea turtles –
poets laying egg-poems
on the beach

o how many little creatures
born of these egg-poems
won't become turtles

Mazunte, Oaxaca
September 3, 2012

o full Moon
your plant your feet of light
among the tomatoes
in the garden – gobbets
of blood and silver

o full Moon
grand silver platter
promise in the sky
a small child's dream
tiny celestial rabbit

June 23, 2013

each cantaloupe slice
a sweet smile
of the Sun

your flashing blink of Sun –
o sunflower lighting up
the field at midday

oh milpas – guardianes
de plumas verdes parados
junto a girasoles
guardianes protectores
de melones contra insectos

5 de julio de 2013

esperanzados –
orientados al futuro
no al pasado

libres, ligeros
sueltos como sueños –
niebla en montañas

9 de julio de 2013

el Sol
nos bendice
con su luz

la Luna
nos bendice
con su amor

28 de julio de 2013

como los sueños
el monte se desgaja –
el pueblo *La Pintada*
es ahora otra *Comala*
lleno de muertos vivos

21 de septiembre de 2013

o corn stalks – green plumed
guardians standing
together with sunflowers
protecting guardians
of melons against insects

July 5, 2013

hope-driven –
facing the future
not the past

free, light-footed
unfettered like dreams –
mist atop mountains

July 9, 2013

the Sun
blesses us
with his light

the Moon
blesses us
with her love

July 28, 2013

like dreams
the mountain falls apart –
the town of *La Pintada**
is now another *Comala*
full of folks buried alive

September 21, 2013

La Pintada is a small town in Guerrero, Mexico, where a mountain slide covered most of the town when families were dining, celebrating Mexican Independence Day on September 16, 2013. 68 people were immediately buried alive under the mud, a tragic result of hurricane Manuel. "Comala" is a town full of living ghosts that appears in the narrative of Mexican writer Juan Rulfo.

a los Escritores del Nuevo Sol	*for the Writers of the New Sun*
llega el torrencial con truenos anunciando la tierna estación otoñal – poetas bajo un tejabán comparten poemas brasas	the torrential rain arrives announcing with thunder the tender season of Fall – poets beneath a patio roof share glowing ember-poems
20 de septiembre de 2013	*September 20, 2013*
en la Torre de Oro con mi bisabuela bailé una sevillana – "soy del Barrio de Santa Cruz" me dice con acento andaluz	on the Gold Tower of Seville I danced with my great-grandmother – with an Andalusian lilt she tells me "I'm from *el Barrio de Santa Cruz*"
2 de noviembre de 2013	*November 2, 2013*
hace mucho Sol pero en mí hay torrencial – girasol de agua	it is very sunny but within me it rains torrents– sunflower of water
4 de noviembre de 2013	*November 4, 2013*
los árboles de mi casa lloran lágrimas ocres – una ardilla para furtiva atisba el cielo luego busca amparo	trees around my house weep ochre tears – a squirrel pauses furtively observes the sky then looks for shelter

oh madera de la vida
fluyendo a la deriva
por el río del tiempo

8 de noviembre de 2013

ramas de árboles
lloran en silencio
con la lluvia otoñal

21 de noviembre de 2013

el Sol danza entre
nubarrones de lluvia –
oh pirámides del cielo

Teotihuacan, México
1 de diciembre de 2013

en la peor sequía
jamás en California
nopales sonríen

9 de enero de 2014

sobre arena
los pájaros escriben
sentidos poemas

listo estoy
para zarpar, pescar
hallarme en el mar

12 de enero de 2014

o driftwood of life
running wild downstream
on the river of time

November 8, 2013

tree branches
weep so quietly
with the autumn rain

November 21, 2013

the Sun dances
amid rain loaded clouds –
o sky pyramids

Teotihuacan, Mexico
December 1, 2013

nopales just smile
amid the worst drought
ever in California

January 9, 2014

on beach sand
birds go on writing
touching poems

I am ready
to sail, fish, find
myself in the sea

January 12, 2014

una ceiba viva
es mi madre – baluarte
de buena voluntad –
cuando otros me negaban
ella se paró a abrazarme

6 de febrero de 2014

Mamá y yo entramos
al mar – ella tiene 90 años –
tomados de manos
ante olas que nos baten – ¿quién
de verdad sostiene a quién?

Nuevo Vallarta, México
18 de abril de 2014

como la luz del sol
el aire, las estrellas, sin
fronteras la poesía

8 de agosto de 2014

a living ceiba
is my mother – a tower
of strength and goodwill –
when others disowned me
she stood up to embrace me

February 6, 2014

Mom and I enter
the sea – she's 90 years old –
we hold hands as waves
come crushing on us – I wonder
who is truly holding whom?

Nuevo Vallarta, Mexico
April 18, 2014

like sunlight
air, stars in the sky
poetry has no borders

August 8, 2014

Como agua enamorada

a todos los poetas y activistas defensores de la vida
tras ver la foto de un tronco en el Río Americano,
Sacramento, California

como	como	como
un árbol	tieso hueso	oscuras piedras
desnudo	del deseo	endurecidas
despojado	de la última	por la ignominia
de todo	ave llorona	la ignorancia
verdor	del alrededor	el terror
como	como	como
un postrado	puente roto	el mundo ciego
luchador	trampolín	que ya ve
sobre arena	esta plegaria	la otra orilla
con hondo	desoída para curar	con ojos de
dolor	del Río Jordán	niño soñador
como	como	como
un Cristo	espejo azul	dulce agua
redentor	de lágrimas	tan enamorada
con brazos	derramadas	del cielo
suplicantes	por nubes solas	del viento
de amor	en clamor	del ardor
¡por la vida!	¡por la vida!	¡por la vida!

9 de enero de 2010

Like Water in Love

to all poets and activists – defenders of life
after a photo of a tree trunk on the American River,
Sacramento, California

like
a naked
tree

robbed
of all its
greenness

like
a wrestler
fallen down

in the arena
in deep
pain

like
a redeeming
Christ

with open
pleading arms
full of love

for all life!

like
a tough to crack
wishbone

of the last
weeping bird
all around

like
a broken bridge
a diving board

this unheard
Jordan River
healing prayer

like
a blue mirror
of fire tears

shed by
lone clouds
in clamor

for all life!

like
dark stones
hardened

by ignominy
ignorance
terror

like
the blind world
that now sees

the other shore
with the dreaming
eyes of a child

like
sweet water
so enamored

with the sky
the wind
the zeal

for all life!

January 9, 2010

Whale Songs

we have no one
but each other

this long night
is overtaking us

we're whales
singing all alone

in this dark sea
trying to find

each other
in this big storm

o we're singing
about blue skies

about bountiful
satisfying times

about rubbing
bodies and tails

o they got us
right this time

we're harpooned
we're going down

falling straight
down in a pool

of warm blood
singing as we fall

brothers, sisters
ram their ships

make them pay
for this blood

they're pulling us
up to their decks

we see their greed
on the long knives

we're not yet dead
but we're being cut

into pieces, we sing
our last whale songs

seagulls are plucking
both of our open eyes

o Father Sun, take
us into your hands

o Mother Sea, guard
the entrails they toss

discard to the waves
o ancient whales

of the Arizona sea
desert, we call out

for your mighty
healing powers

make our nation
whole again

a welcoming
open sea to all

o sky whales
o sea whales

o land whales
o spirit whales

o whales
from the past

o whales
from the future

we call out
for you to undo

the wounds
they've done

set us free
all unharmed

we'll praise
sing forever

the precious
gifts of this sky

of this land
this vast sea

that's always
been ours

Tucson, Arizona
May 30, 2010

Árbol

hay un árbol
muy frondoso
en mi vida

con ramas
extendidas
apuntando

al cielo
con raíces
muy hondas

enterradas
en el alma
de la Tierra

un árbol
muy estoico
amigo mío

que mudo
me aconseja
muy sabio

un árbol
amor mío
de mi vida

1 de marzo de 2011

Tree

there is a tree
lush and leafy
in my life

with extended
branches
pointing

to the sky
with very
deep roots

buried
in the soul
of the Earth

a tree
very stoic
friend of mine

that mutely
advises me
full of wisdom

a tree
dearest love
of my life

March 1, 2011

Poetas puentes

poetas puentes
no reconocen
fronteras

poetas puentes
tienen poemarios
como pasaporte

poetas puentes
extienden
los brazos

cruzan túneles
poéticos fuera
de la ley

escriben versos
que dan visas
a perpetuidad

hasta formar
puentes humanos
sobre ríos

son mariposas
migrantes
de la palabra

son arañas
que tienden
telarañas

poetas puentes
componen
poemas puentes –

catecúmbenos
que se reúnen
a plena luz

con seda
tan fina como
los suspiros

del mundo
son el alma
el corazón

Tijuana, Baja California Norte
12 de agosto de 2012

Bridge Poets

bridge poets
don't recognize
borders

bridge poets
have chapbooks
as passports

bridge poets
extend
their arms

they cross
outlaw poetic
tunnels

they write verses
granting them
life-long visas

until forming
human bridges
over rivers

they are migrant
butterflies
of the word

they are spiders
weaving
their webs

bridge poets
compose
bridge poems –

catacomb goers
who meet
in broad day

with silk
as fine as
sighs

they are the soul
the heart of
the world

Tijuana, Baja California Norte
August 12, 2012

Kritya

poema/carta a Rati Saxena,
organizadora del Festival Internacional de Poesía – Kritya 2012
Trivandrum en Kerala, India, el 16 al 19 de enero de 2012

"Kritya"
shabd shakti
oh poder de las palabras

te fallé, *"Kritya"*
dejé que el silencio
me venciera

y la desesperanza
me desenraizara
me arrastrara

como un gran
árbol de caoba
por la selva tropical

porque gente
como yo no merece
misericordia

porque yo no tengo
puerto protector
ni patria real

desheredado
por familia
por colegas

mi destino está
en manos
de extraños

desconocidos –
mis verdaderos
compatriotas

"Kritya"
shabd shakti
oh poder de las palabras

no pude escapar
de esta imponente
prisión de palabras

si tuve alguna vez
la llave abre puertas
la he perdido

en vez de unirme
a los poetas venidos
de todo el mundo

a encender
la lámpara ceremonial
al inicio de *"Kritya"*

el Festival Internacional
de Poesía de Trivandrum
en Kerala, India

yo intenté prender
palabras contra
la prohibición

de libros escritos
por autores nativos
y chicanos/as

de aulas
escolares en
Tucson, Arizona

"Kritya"
shabd shakti
oh poder de las palabras

al mediodía
cuando mi poemas
estaban programados

para volar como
mariposas sin fronteras
en español, inglés

y malayalam
en el primer día
de *"Kritya"*

este poeta escribía
un haiku/sueño para
Martin Luther King, Jr.

"toda la humanidad
llendo libre, sin obstáculos
como ríos al mar"

miles de millas
al otro lado del mundo
de Trivandrum

soñando/invocando
el poder de las palabra
en el Kutiyattam

sintiendo la poesía
en solidaridad fluyendo
junto al río Poorna

4 de febrero de 2012

Kritya

poem/letter to Rati Saxena
organizer of the International Poetry Festival – Kritya 2012
Trivandrum in Kerala, India, on January 16 – 19, 2012

"Kritya"
shabd shakti
o power of words

I failed you, *Kritya*
I allowed silence
to overcome me

despair
uprooted me
dragged me

like a big
mahogany tree
in the rainforest

for people
like me deserve
no mercy

for I have
no safe haven
nor real country

disowned
by family
by peers

my fate held
by the hands
of complete

strangers –
my true
countrymen

"Kritya"
shabd shakti
o power of words

I couldn't escape
this imposing
prison of words

if I ever had
the opening key
I lost it

instead of joining
the poets from all
over the world

in lighting
the ceremonial lamp
at the start of *"Kritya"*

the International Poetry
Festival at Trivandrum
in Kerala, India

I tried lighting
words against
the banning

of books written
by Native and
Chicano/authors

from school
classrooms
in Tucson, Arizona

"Kritya"
shabd shakti
o power of words

at noon
with my poems
scheduled to fly

as borderless
butterflies in
Spanish, English

and Malayalam
on the first day
of *"Kritya"*

this poet was writing
a dream/haiku for
Martin Luther King, Jr.

"all humanity
running unimpeded
like rivers to the sea"

thousands of miles
half a world away
from Trivandrum

dreaming/invoking
the power of words
in the Kutiyattam

sensing poetry
solidarity running
alongside Poorna river

February 4, 2012

Bahía de Banderas

levantamos
banderas
junto al mar

ofrendas
de amate
para el Sol

mariposas
multicolores
para engalanar

todo el valle
y la bahía
como collar

de jade
turquesa
y coral

un tocado
de plumas
de quetzal —

danzamos
día y noche
sin parar

la Luna —
tortilla
celestial

nos sirve
de guía
magistral

un tambor
nos marca
el compás

Bahía de Banderas

we raise
flags along
the seashore

bark paper
offerings
for the Sun

multicolored
butterflies
to embellish

the whole
valley and bay
as a necklace

of jade
turquoise
and coral

a headdress
of quetzal
feathers —

we dance
day and night
nonstop

the Moon —
celestial
tortilla

serves us
as a masterful
guide

a drum
beats out
the rhythm

los pasos	the steps
de nuestro	of our
corazón –	heart –
cuando	as we set
las banderas	the flags
encendemos	on fire
antorchas	torches
luciérnagas	fireflies
de la noche	of the night
todos	we all
elevamos	raise up
un canto	a song
junto con	together with
columnas de	columns of smoke
humo al cielo –	to the sky –
nos volvemos	we turn
nubes	into clouds
estrellas	stars
aquí alrededor	around here
nativos somos	we are Natives
otra vez	once again

Puerto Vallarta, Jalisco   *Puerto Vallarta, Jalisco*
22 de agosto de 2012   *August 22, 2012*

Ballena

aquí soy
una ballena
jorobada

entonando
un canto
del alma

26 de agosto de 2012

Whale

here I am
a humpback
whale

singing
a soulful
song

August 26, 2012

Iguana

en la noche
de la iguana
muchas moscas
gran festín

26 de agosto de 2012

Iguana

in the night
of the iguana
many flies
great feast

August 26, 2012

Relámpago

raíz
del cielo
sobre la tierra

árbol
de luz
en la oscuridad

que dura
un instante
una eternidad

anunciando
un tamboreo
celestial

26 de agosto de 2012

Lightning

a root
of the sky
upon the land

a tree
of light
in the dark

lasting
an instant
an eternity

announcing
a celestial
drumming

August 26, 2012

Puesta de Sol

el Cielo
el Mar
el Sol

hacen
un *ménage*
a trois

amoroso
al final
del día

el Sol
acariciando
muslos

el mar
besando
el Cielo

la playa
es el lecho
el lienzo

que enmarca
el principio
y el final

el Alfa
y el Omega
juntos

uniendo
el primer
y último día

el manazo
y llanto del
recién nacido

Sunset

the Sky
the Sea
the Sun

make
a *ménage*
a trois

amorous
at the end
of the day

the Sun
caressing
thighs

the Sea
kissing
the Sky

the beach
is the bed
the canvas

framing
the beginning
and the end

the Alpha
and the Omega
altogether

uniting
the first
and last day

the slap
and the cry
of the new born

el santo	the holy
óleo del	ointment
agonizante	of the dying
las brasas	the embers
y las cenizas	and the ashes
del amor	of love
el *Big Bang*	the Big Bang
su instantánea	its instantaneous
inflación	inflation
y el último	and the last
suspiro	solar
solar –	sigh –
ballenas	humpback
jorobadas	whales gather
se concentran	together
en el cielo	in the sky
para despedir	in farewell
al Sol	to the Sun
convertido	turned into
en un corazón	the heart
de dinosaurio	of a dinosaur
que sangra	bleeding
hasta enrojecer	until redding
el horizonte	the horizon
el Cielo	the Sky
la Tierra	the Earth
el Mar	the Sea
se incendian	ignite until
hasta apagar	extinguishing
la antorcha	the torch
del Sol	of the Sun
entre los cerros	amid hillsides
de Punta Mitla	at Mitla Point

oh *Mitla*
Mictlan – Tierra
de los Ancestros

ahora soy
un pelícano
ciego

dispuesto
a pescar
en la oscuridad

oh hermanos
compartimos
la misma

locura de todos
los elementos
que lloran

la muerte
súbita de
Papá Sol

y esperan
su regreso
su resurrección

Bucerías, Nayarit
14 de septiembre de 2011

o *Mitla*
Mictlan – Land
of our Ancestors

I am now
a blind
pelican

ready
to fish
in the dark

o brothers
we share
the same

madness of all
the elements
weeping for

the sudden
death of
Father Sun

awaiting
his return
his resurrection

Bucerías, Nayarit
September 14, 2011

Cuatro direcciones

cuatro templos
hay en el centro
geodésico de
Monte Albán

subo al Templo
del Norte/Tierra
para honrar
a los ancestros

invoco *"Tahui"*
a los cuatro vientos,
los montes y valles
del alrededor:

Etla al Norte
Oaxaca al Este
Zimatlán al Sur
Tlacolula al Oeste

desde el Templo
del Sur/Agua
diviso los campos
fértiles de Oaxaca

cruzo las dos
columnas de piedra
del Templo del
Oeste/Viento

me pongo a orar
para aliviar el dolor
de la humanidad
y bendecir el mundo

Monte Albán, Oaxaca
19 de agosto de 2012

Four Directions

there are four
temples in
the geodesic center
of Monte Albán

I climb the Temple
of the North/Earth
to pay homage
to our ancestors

I call forth *"Tahui"*
to the four winds,
to the mountains
and valleys all around:

Etla to the North
Oaxaca to the East
Zimatlán to the South
Tlacolula to the West

from the Temple
of the South/Water
I can see the green
fields of Oaxaca

I cross the two
stone columns
of the Temple
of the West/Wind

I start praying
to soothe the pain
of all humanity
and bless the world

Monte Albán, Oaxaca
August 19, 2012

Juego de pelota

la pelota
es el Sol

la cancha
el universo

el eje es
Norte-Sur

nuestra vida
un punto

equidistante
entre

la vida
y la muerte

Monte Albán, Oaxaca
19 de agosto de 2012

Ball Game

the Sun
is the ball

the universe
the ball court

the axis is
North-South

our life
a point

equidistant
between

life
and death

Monte Albán, Oaxaca
August 19, 2012

Mitla

Mitla es
un poema

nubes
de agua

labrado
en piedra

mariposas
en glifos

cierro
los ojos

danzan
en piedra

abro
los oídos

mis manos
quieren

oigo
muros

acariciar
las piedras

recitando
versos

las mejores
de esta tierra

huelo
el dulce

como solía
acariciar

humo
de copal

las mejillas
de mi abuela

Mitla, Oaxaca
21 de agosto de 2012

Mitla

Mitla is
a poem

crafted
in stone

I close
my eyes

open
my ears

hear
walls

reciting
verses

I smell
the sweet

copal
smoke

water
clouds

butterfly
glyphs

dance
in stones

my hands
want

to caress
the stones

the finest
of this land

as I used
to caress

my grandma's
cheeks

Mitla, Oaxaca
August 21, 2012

En Totontepec

manantial:
espejo del cielo
paraíso ancestral

las montañas
bendicen todo
con vida y color

mantra poética:
nada, nadie
nunca —

todo
todos
siempre

el poeta
y el mundo:

el ciego
no ve

el sordo
no oye

pero así
el mudo

habla
al mundo

de un modo
como poeta

Totontepec Villa de Morelos, Oaxaca
25 de agosto de 2012

In Totontepec

water spring:
sky mirror
ancestral paradise

the mountains
bless everything
with life and color

poetic mantra:
nothing, nobody
never —

everything
everybody
always

the poet
and the world:

the blind
doesn't see

the deaf
doesn't hear

and yet
the mute

speaks
to the world

somehow
as poet

Totontepec Villa de Morelos, Oaxaca
August 25, 2012

Ninguneo

no estoy
ni estuve
aquí jamás

no hago
ni hice nada
tampoco

soy nadie
un cero a
la izquierda

no dejo
huellas
ni rastros

solo
un hilo de
puntos rojos –

una rosa
en la boca
me hace sangrar

Totontepec Villa de Morelos, Oaxaca
26 de agosto de 2012

Shunning

I am not
nor was I
ever here

I don't do
nor did I do
anything either

I am nobody
a zero digit
to the left

I don't leave
prints, hints
nor traces

only
a line of
red dots –

a rose in
in my mouth
makes me bleed

Totontepec Villa de Morelos, Oaxaca
August 26, 2012

Noche oaxaqueña

la noche	la noche
se abre	florece
como puerta	como flor
tras la lluvia	el agua
torrencial	se vierte
de la tarde	de un cántaro
Venus brilla	de barro
en el horizonte	negro
del Oeste	a otro –
ahora somos	sí, somos
asteroides	delfines
perdidos	acarreando
en la franja	su amor
entre Marte	en la punta
y la Tierra	de su nariz

Huatulco, Oaxaca
29 de agosto de 2012

Oaxacan Night

night
opens up
like a door

after
the torrential rain
of the evening

Venus shines
on the East
horizon

now we are
some lost
asteroids

in the belt
between Mars
and Earth

night
blooms
like a flower

spring water
pours
from

a black
clay jug
to another –

yes, we are
dolphins
hauling

their love
on the points
of their noses

Huatulco, Oaxaca
29 de agosto de 2012

Barca-poema	Boat-Poem
horizonte	boundless
sin límite	horizon of
de mar	the sea
ola por	wave about
reventar	to break
y mojar	and soak
la blanca	the white
arena de	sands of
la página	the page
ala de	wing of
gaviota	a seagull
en vuelo	in flight
nubarrón	dark cloud
anunciando	announcing
lluvia	rain
barca-poema	boat-poem
a la deriva	adrift
sin vela	without sail
sin remos	without oars
sin puerto	without harbor
donde anclar	where to anchor

Puerto Escondido, Oaxaca
5 de septiembre de 2012

Puerto Escondido, Oaxaca
September 5, 2012

Verde	Green
Oaxaca es verde	Oaxaca is green
todo verde	all green
verde quelite	wild herb green
verde húmedo	damp green
verde lluvia	rain green
verde feliz	happy green
verde niñez	childhood green
verde maíz	corn green
verde Cocijo*	*Cocijo*** green

25 de agosto de 2012

August 25, 2012

*Cocijo: Deidad zapoteca de la lluvia, trueno y relámpagos que corresponde a Tláloc del México central y Chaac de la civilización maya.

**Cocijo: Zapotec diety of rain, thunder and lightning that corresponds to Tlaloc of Central Mexico and Chaac in the Maya civilization.

Tsunami

tras el terremoto de 8.9
puntos Richter en Japón
el 11 de marzo de 2011

alas del mar
furiosas revuelcan
lágrimas con brisa

el agua incendia
edificios, casas huérfanas
arden de pena

olas de dolor
barren todo el Pacífico –
la Tierra es una

la noche cae –
oscurece dondequiera y
los gatos salen

cópulos de nieve
lloran los destrozos
costeros del Japón

el silencio es roto
solo por el sollozo
de árboles

un cerezo solo
se alista a florecer
entre tanta pena

aquí las lágrimas
no caen más al suelo
flotan al cielo
como nuevos luceros –
diamantes de memorias

Tsunami

after Japan's 8.9
Richter points earthquake
on March 11, 2011

the furious wings
of the sea mixing
tears with mist

water sets fire to
buildings, orphaned houses
burning in sorrow

waves of grief
sweep all of the Pacific –
the Earth is one

night falls –
darkness everywhere
as cats come out

falling snow weeps
for the destroyed
coasts of Japan

silence is broken
only by the sobbing
of the trees

a lone cherry tree
gets ready to bloom
amid so much doom

here tears no longer
fall to the ground
they float to the sky
like new night stars –
diamonds made of memories

Plegaria urgente

*tras el desastre de la planta
nuclear de Fukushima en Japón*

desarma estas bombas vivas
de reactores, Madre Tierra
¡tennos piedad!

como niños tontos
jugamos con el fuego
hasta quemar todo

*¡Toci Tonantzin!
¡Citlacueye! ¡Tlazolteotl!
¡tla Tlatecuhtli!*

24 de marzo de 2011

Urgent Prayer

*after the Fukushima nuclear
plant disaster in Japan*

disarm these ticking bombs
called reactors, Mother Earth
have mercy on us!

we foolish children
who recklessly play with fire
are getting all burned

*Toci Tonantzin!
Citlacueye! Tlazolteotl!
tla Tlatecuhtli!*

March 24, 2011

Para las Filipinas tras el Tifón Yolanda

luego del gran vacío
dejado por Yolanda, hoy
todos somos filipinos

bajo la noche
nos besamos como amantes
supervivientes

que el Sol filipino
surja y dé otra vez calor
y esperanza a todos

12 de noviembre de 2013

¿está lloviendo
o llora el mundo entero
de luto aún?

25 de noviembre de 2013

no más lágrimas –
ahora aliento humano para
las noches solas

sosteniendo
a la Tierra y a todos –
el espíritu humano

28 de diciembre de 2013

For the Philippines After Typhoon Yolanda

in the wake of great void
left by Yolanda, we are now
all Filipinos

under the cover of night
we kiss like lovers
like survivors

may the Filipino Sun
surge up again and give
warmth and hope for all

November 12, 2013

is it raining
or is the whole world weeping
still in mourning?

November 25, 2013

no more tears –
now human breath for
lonely nights

sustaining the Earth
together and everyone –
the human spirit

December 28, 2013

Hay(Na)Ku filipino

tras los poetas Vince Gotera
y Eileen Tabios

azul
azul filipino
lleno de esperanza

Sol
Sol filipino
brillando para todos

nunca
todos solos –
nosotros con ustedes

sin
importar distancias –
siempre con ustedes

pensando en ustedes
como familia
juntos

26 de noviembre de 2013

Filipino Hay(Na)Ku

after poets Vince Gotera
and Eileen Tabios

blue
Filipino blue
full of hope

Sun
Filipino Sun
shining for all

never
all alone –
we're with you

despite
the distances –
always with you

thinking of you
as family
together

November 26, 2013

Vince Gotera writes: *"The HAY(NA)KU is a poetic form invented by Filipino poet Eileen Tabios. It's a word-counting three-line form: 1 word in line 1, 2 words in line 2, 3 words in line 3. Sometimes also in reverse: 3 words in line 1, 2 words in line 2, 1 word in line 3. Reverse haiku can be used for emphasis or for a change in the dynamics and movement of a poem. The form depends on good lineation ... not just the division of six-word groups into the line pattern, but actually useful, sense-laden line breaks."*

Azul sin fronteras

azul
como el mar
al amanecer

azul
como el cielo
al atardecer

azul
como la tristeza
la soledad

azul
como la esperanza
la felicidad

azul
sin fronteras
unificador

azul
como el puntito
azul

visto
desde la lejanía
sideral –

la Tierra
joya reluciente
azul

entre
la vasta
oscuridad

28 de julio de 2013

Borderless Blue

blue
like the sea
at dawn

blue
like the sky
at dusk

blue
like sadness
loneliness

blue
like hope
happiness

bonding
borderless
blue

blue
like the little
blue dot

seen
from afar
in outer space –

the Earth
shining
blue jewel

amid
the vast
darkness

July 28, 2013

IV Aire / Air

el aleteo	the wing flapping
de mariposas puede	of butterflies can cause
causar un huracán	a hurricane

Curanderos

una estrella fugaz
cae en medio de la nada –
como poema cura

6 de enero de 2011

nunca seamos balas
sino manos que curan
heridas que sangran

huyamos de leones
y águilas, contentos siempre
de ser mariposas

seamos velas
prendidas dando luz
en la oscuridad

a Daniel Hernández Jr.

ningún héroe, dice –
gentil, humilde, valiente
como héroe real

el viento sopló
pero la hoja del árbol
no besó la tierra

¡ella abrió los ojos! –
que este milagro nos abra
los ojos a todos

desde esa Arena
el Sol de Arizona derrite
el hielo invernal

9 de enero de 2011

Healers

a shooting star falls
in the middle of nowhere –
it's a healing poem

January 6, 2011

let us never be
bullets but hands that heal
bleeding wounds

let us flee lions
and eagles, always content
to be butterflies

let us be lit candles
giving caring light
in the darkness

to Daniel Hernández Jr.

not a heroe at all, he says –
just kind, humble, valiant
like a real heroe

the wind blew
but the lone leaf on the tree
did not kiss the ground

she opened her eyes! –
may this miracle open
the eyes of us all

from that Arena
the Arizona Sun melts
wintertime ice

January 9, 2011

flor primaveral –
llama viva de color
solo un instante
celebrando la vida.
en desafío a la muerte

9 de junio de 2011

poder de la verdad –
paz, justicia, armonía
de noción y acción

3 de abril de 2012

comprometidos
a reducir toda aflicción
como podamos

27 de julio de 2012

oh Luna llena –
a las almas de octubre
con tu luz cubre

29 de octubre de 2012

oh Sol Flor guíanos
con tu luz a la Nueva Era
este Solsticio Invernal

10 de noviembre de 2012

Spring flower –
flame alive with color
just a mere instant
celebrating life
in defiance of death

June 9, 2011

the power of truth –
peace, justice, harmony
in thought and deed

April 3, 2012

we are committed
to reducing as much
suffering we can

July 27, 2012

o full Moon –
with your light cover
the souls of October

October 29, 2012

o Flower Sun guide us
with your light to the New Era
this Winter Solstice

November 10, 2012

*Xochitonatiuh
in tonalli in yollotl
in tlanextia*

Flor Sol
en alma y corazón
siempre brillando

Flower Sun
in our soul and heart
always shining

mariposas, campos
abejas, flores – todos
notas de un canto

13 de noviembre de 2012

nieva en silencio –
la Sierra Nevada es
novia en blanco

todos los árboles
dan gracias vivas
al calor del Sol

gracias le damos
al don de la Palabra –
regalo y cura de luz

gaviota en vuelo –
entre ala, pico y mar
nos traes al Sol

oh, escuchemos
la luz de las estrellas –
"¡somos solo uno!"

22 de noviembre de 2012

hojas caen –
los árboles susurran
suave a la Tierra

24 de noviembre de 2012

llueve muy quedo –
suspiros líquidos caen
hechos lágrimas

butterflies, fields
bees, flowers – all
notes of one song

November 13, 2012

snowing in silence –
the Sierra Nevada is
a bride in white

all the trees
give living thanks
to the warmth of the Sun

thanks we give
to the blessing of the Word –
gift and cure of light

seagull in flight –
in your wing, beak, and sea
you bring us the Sun

o, let us listen
to the light of stars –
"we are just one"

November 22, 2012

leaves fall –-
the trees murmur
softly to the Earth

November 24, 2012

so quietly it rains –
liquid sighs made tears
fall on the ground

el Sol vencerá
la larga noche invernal –
oh preciosa luz

oh colibrí de luz
entre nubes en vuelo –
flor del cielo

2 de diciembre de 2012

Papá Sol entra
por el portón, sonriendo
canta con nosotros

el Sol es un niño
bajando la pirámide
de Chichen Iztá

oh Flor Sol –
no anuncias un mundo final
sino uno inicial

una nueva era
una nueva conciencia humana
un renacimiento

oh dulce perfume
de justicia, tolerancia
compasión, armonía

oh nueva flor
brotando en el corazón
de la humanidad

*Solsticio Invernal
21 de diciembre de 2012*

en invierno, las ramas
son raíces al aire
rogando al cielo

the Sun will vanquish
the long Winter night –
o precious light

o hummingbird of light
among clouds in flight –
flower of the sky

December 2, 2012

Father Sun comes through
the wide door, beaming
he sings with us

the Sun is a kid
dashing down the pyramid
of Chichen Itzá

o Flower Sun –
you don't announce a world's end
but the start of a new one

a new era
a new human consciousness
a renaissance

o sweet perfume
of justice, tolerance
compassion, harmony

o new flower
springing up in the heart
of humanity

*Wnter Solstice
December 21, 2012*

in Winter, tree branches
turn into open air roots
pleading to the sky

un árbol humano
con brazos abiertos –
un sueño expansivo

1 de enero de 2013

herido y solo
con sabor a ceniza –
silencio abrumador

14 de enero de 2013

oh manos ciegas
sordas, mudas, sangrientas
sin corazón –
causa de tantas muertes
en la frontera al Sur

tenue luz doquier –
la ternura de extraños
colma vacíos

2 de julio de 2013

pintamos la casa
verde cobre mohoso como
la Estatua de la Libertad –
en su vientre nos sentimos
libres como quetzales en vuelo

7 de agosto de 2013

¡vivan los muertos! –
cempasúchiles los guíen
el Día de Muertos

2 de noviembre de 2013

one human tree
with wide open arms –
an expansive dream

January 1, 2013

wounded and alone
with this taste of ashes –
overwhelming silence

January 14, 2013

o blind, deaf, mute
heartless bloody hands –
cause of so many
deaths on the border
to the South

soft light everywhere–
the tenderness of strangers
fills up the voids

July 2, 2013

we're painting our home
tarnished copper green like
the Statue of Liberty –
in her bosom we'll feel free
as quetzal birds in full flight

August 7, 2013

long life to the dead! –
may marigolds guide you
on the Day of the Dead

November 2, 2013

vuela, vuela
pajarito hasta más allá
de la estratósfera

9 de noviembre de 2013

oh flores somos
tan tiernos, tan amorosos
tan temporales

gracias universales –
gracias, luz y oscuridad
¡gracias a todos!

28 de noviembre de 2013

con Mandela
toda África sonreía
abierta al porvenir

8 de diciembre 2013

la locura cura –
la flor y el canto curan
cuerpo y alma

la vida es una flor
que dura solo un día
en la oscuridad

la noche – manto
de nuestra diaria muerte
y resurrección

19 de diciembre 2013

todas las noches
nos morimos soñando
un sueño vivo

21 de diciembre de 2013

fly, fly, little bird
until you reach beyond
the stratosphere

November 9, 2013

o flowers we are
so tender, so loving
so ephemeral

universal thanks –
thanks, light and darkness
thank you all!

November 28, 2013

with Mandela
all Africa smiled
openly at the future

December 8, 2013

madness heals –
flower and song heal
body and soul

life is a flower
lasting just a day
through the darkness

night – dark shroud
of our daily death
and resurrection

December 19, 2013

every night
we die dreaming
a living dream

December 21, 2013

la vida es sueño
la vida es flor, canto
la vida es el poema real

el poeta/*tlacuilo*
pinta poemas con alas
para así volar

¿quién hace poesía?
poetas no escriben poesía –
¡la poesía los "escribe"!

28 de diciembre de 2013

cada estrella
una luciérnaga
soñando el cosmos

al final
el universo oscuro
soñará sin luz

1 de enero de 2014

life is a dream
life is flower, song
life is the real poem

the poet/*tlacuilo*
paints poems with wings
in order to fly

who writes poetry?
poets don't write poetry –
poetry "writes" them!

December 28, 2013

each star
a firefly dreaming
the cosmos

in the end
the darkened universe
will dream without light

January 1, 2014

Jesús indocumentado

de niño quería correr
al Monte de los Olivos y decir
"Jesús, te van a matar…"

oh, un día, Jesús
te bendecimos con palmas
y otro, te damos cruz

te he visto, Jesús
por Jerusalén y Nueva York
cargando tu cruz

tres clavos sin piedad
de no importarnos los demás
punzan tus manos y pies

hoy, buen Jesús
te quiero desclavar
y bajar de esta cruz –

Jesús se llama
Roberto, Miguel, Anabel
en la cárcel sin ningún papel

cempasúchiles en vez
de coronas de espinas
para tu pueblo, Jesús

que flores, buena voluntad
deshagan los nudos ciegos
de alambres de púas

22 de marzo de 2013

Undocumented Jesus

as I child I wanted to run
to the Mount of Olives and warn
"Jesus, they're going to kill you…"

o, Jesus, one day
we bless you with palms
another, we crucify you

I've seen you, Jesus
in Jerusalem and New York
carrying your cross

three merciless nails
of not caring for others
pierce your hands and feet

today, good Jesus
I want to un-nail you
take you down from this cross –

Jesus is named
Roberto, Miguel, Anabel
in jail with no papers

marigolds instead
of crowns of thorns
for your people, Jesus

may flowers, good will
undo the blind knots
of barbed wire borders

March 22, 2013

Compasión sin fronteras

qué tal si fueras *Chava*
un joven niño de 11 años
de un barrio a las afueras

de la ciudad capital
de El Salvador, de los más
pobres de los pobres

y tu papá cuyo propio
padre había sido muerto
en la calle por el ejército

durante la guerra civil
de los años 1980s cuando
él también solo tenía 11 años

decide irse un día
a buscar suerte al *Norte*
y les promete a ti

y a tu mamá
que le mandará mucha
plata que nunca llega

forzando a tu mamá
a irse a buscar una mejor
vida en California –

tú lloras de noche
porque no has visto
a tu mamá en 5 años

ella se está volviendo
un fantasma, una lejana voz
en el teléfono de un vecina

tu mamá, te dice que
no arriesgues tu propia vida
uniéndote a los miles

Borderless Compassion

what if you were *Chava*
a 11 years old young boy
from the outskirts

of the capital city
of El Salvador, among
the poorest of the poor

and your *Papa* whose own
father had been killed
on the street by the military

during the civil war
in the 1980s when he was
also only 11 years old

decides one day
to take off to *El Norte*
and promises you

and your *Mama*
that he will send plenty
of dough that never arrives

forcing your *Mama* to leave
in search for a better
life in California –

you weep at night
because you haven't seen
your *Mama* in five years

she is becoming a ghost
a fainting voice coming off
a neighbor's cell phone

she tells you not to come
not to risk your own life
by joining the thousands

de niños que se van al *Norte*
pero una mara local acaba
de matar a tu mejor amigo

te dicen que tú eres el siguiente –
tú no tienes otra opción
que llamar a miembros

familiares y amigos
para que te presten dinero
para el viaje al *Norte* –

qué tal si tú fueras uno
de los niños migrantes que
vienen de Centroamérica

escapando de este ciclo cruel
de violencia y muerte
sosteniendo sus vidas

y sus sueños
en sus pequeñas manos
deseando arriesguiarlo todo

anhelando unirse
a sus amorosas familias
volviéndose en refugiados

mariposas migrantes
atrapadas en un mundo que
precisa compasión sin fronteras

el muro más duro –
un corazón amurallado
sin compasión

4 de julio de 2014

---

of children going North
but the local *mara* gang
just killed your best friend

you're told you're next –
you have no option
but to call all family

relatives and friends
to lend you the money
for the journey North –

what if you were one
of the migrant kids arriving
from Central América

escaping this cruel cycle
of violence and death
holding their lives

and their dreams
in their own small hands
willing to risk it all

wishing to join together
with their loving families
becoming true refugees

migrant butterflies
trapped in a world in need
of borderless compassion

the hardest wall of all –
a walled human heart
without compassion

July 4, 2014

Niños refugiados

oh tiernas flores
huyendo de comillos de La Bestia –
que hallen refugio
en brazos que aman, cuidan
protegen a la niñez

6 de julio de 2014

Refugee Children

o tender flowers
fleeing from the fangs of The Beast –
may you find refuge
in the loving, caring arms
protective of all children

July 6, 2014

Si Jesús fuera Papa

si a Jesús
lo eligieran
como Papa

lo primero
que haría
sería dejar

el sacrosanto
vestuario
papal

para andar
en el Vaticano
y dondequiera

en simple
overol azul
de trabajador

abriría
las puertas
de par en par

a las mujeres
para hacerlas
sacerdotas

obispas
arzobispas
y cardenalas

tendría
los brazos
bien abiertos

para abrazar
a la gente más
necesitada

If Jesus Were the Pope

if Jesus
were elected
as Pope

the first thing
he would do
would be to abandon

the pompous
vestments
of popes

go around
in the Vatican
and elsewhere

in the humble
denim overalls
of workers

he would open
the doors
all the way

to women
to make them
priests

bishops
archbishops
and cardinals

he would have
his arms
wide open

to embrace
the people
most in need

ayudando	helping out
a inmigrantes	immigrants
y sus familias	and their families
a nadie	he would not
de antemano	condemn anyone
condenaría	out of hand
a todos y	he would love
todas amaría	everybody
por igual	the same
a homosexuales	gays
lesbianas	lesbians
transgéneros	transgender
blancos	Whites
y morenos	and people of color
sin distinción	without distinction
si a Jesús	if Jesus
lo eligieran	were elected
como Papa	as Pope
se preocuparía	he would see
para que nadie	that nobody
se quedara	was ever left
sin pan	without bread
sin casa	without home
sin educación	without education
pero quizás	but maybe
por ser así	for being this way
al final	at the end
a Jesús	Jesus would
lo volverían	be crucified
a crucificar	once again
11 de febrero de 2013	*February 11, 2013*

Plegaria del pueblo

al Papa Francisco

antes de dar
tu bendición
Urbi et Orbi
blessing

a la Ciudad
Eterna de Roma
y al mundo

como buen latino
pediste la bendición
primero a tu pueblo

así como nosotros
pedimos nos bendigan
nuestros mayores

Francisco –
sé siempre fiel
a tu nombre

que te guíe
el espíritu
de bondad

de paz
de sencillez
de compasión

el ejemplo
de servicio
a los pobres

del humilde
San Francisco
de Asís

People's Prayer

for Pope Francis

before bestowing
your *Urbi et Orbi*
blessing

to the Eternal
City of Rome
and to the world

as a good Latino
you first asked people
for their blessings

just as we ask
our own elders
for their blessings

Francisco –
may you always be
faithful to your name

may you be guided
by the spirit
of kindness

of peace
of simplicity
of compassion

the example
of service
to the poor

of the humble
Saint Francis
of Assisi

Francisco – sé
un papa "católico"
real (universal)

un Papa para todas
las criaturas vivas
de esta Tierra

Francisco – abre
puertas y ventanas
de par en par

al aire fresco
de la Nueva Era
del Sol Flor

(Maradona, Argentina
y toda Latinoamérica
te mandan bendiciones)

13 de marzo de 2013

Francisco – may
you be a real "catholic"
(universal) pope

a Pope for all
living creatures
of this Earth

Francisco – open up
doors and windows
once and for all

to the fresh air
of the New Era
of the Flower Sun

(Maradona, Argentina
and the entire Latin America
send you their blessings)

March 13, 2013

"Now, I would like to give you a blessing, but first I want to ask you for a favor. Before the bishop blesses the people, I ask that you pray to the Lord so that he blesses me. This is the prayer of the people who are asking for the blessing of their bishop… In silence, let us say this prayer of you for me."
    – Pope Francis, from the balcony of the Saint Peter's Basilica Vatican City, March 13, 2013

Seamos todos Gandhi

seamos todos Gandhi
Martin Luther King, Jr.
Nelson Mandela

César Chávez
Dolores Huerta
Rosa Parks

enviados de paz
razón, tolerancia, bondad
no odio, coraje

todos encarcelados
rechazados por el 1%
por sus principios –

de la desesperanza
miedo, dolor, saquemos
gozo, fe y esperanza

seamos todos Nelson Mandela
un pacífico león africano
lamiendo, cuidando, curando

las hondas heridas del apartheid
reemplazando las raíces del odio
con las bondadosas ramas del amor

de un gran frondoso árbol baobab
erguido muy alto hasta el cielo
dando sombra a toda la humanidad

5 de diciembre de 2013

Let Us All Be Gandhi

let us all be Gandhi,
Martin Luther King, Jr.
Nelson Mandela

César Chávez
Dolores Huerta
Rosa Parks

messengers of peace
reason, tolerance, goodwill
not hatred, anger

all jailed at one time
and dismissed by the 1%
for their principles –

from despair
fear, sorrow, let us draw
enjoyment, faith, and hope

let us all be Nelson Mandela
a peaceful African lion
licking, tending, healing

the deep wounds of apartheid
replacing the roots of hatred
with the bountiful branches of love

of a big leafy baobab tree
erect and tall to the sky
providing shade to all humanity

December 5, 2013

Estrellas

estrellas
ocupan
la noche celestial

así como el 99%
ocupan
la atención

demandando
al 1%
por su porción

justa
de luz
en la oscuridad

13 de noviembre de 2013

Stars

stars
occupy
the night sky

just as the 99%
occupy
the spotlight

demanding
the 1%
for their fair

share
of light
in the night

November 13, 2013

Cinco Lorcas

tres clavos
una corona
de espinas

un costado
lacerado
una cruz

un lienzo
una tumba
para Jesús

¡ay! roca
cuerpo
resucitado

¡ay! Lorca
pecho
acribillado

sin tumba
oh campo
florido

un rostro
dos manos
dos pies

cinco Lorcas:
desnudo
radical

soñador
agónico
subliminal

cinco dedos
una mano
cercenada

Five Lorcas

three nails
a crown
of thorns

a pierced
ribcage
a cross

a shroud
a tomb
for Jesus

ay! rock
resuscitated
body

ay! Lorca
bullet-ridden
chest

without grave
o flowering
countryside

a face
two hands
two feet

five Lorcas:
naked
radical

dreamer
agonizing
subliminal

five fingers
an amputated
hand

cinco Lorcas
siempre vivos
en plena luz

11 de abril de 2013

five Lorcas
forever alive
in broad daylight

April 11, 2013

Dulce barrio

toda La Misión
tiene olor fraternal
a panadería

por eso aquí
la gente lleva pan dulce
como corazón

La Misión, San Francisco
10 de enero de 2014

Sweet Barrio

the entire Mission
has the fraternal aroma
of Mexican bakeries

that's why here
people have *pan dulce*
for hearts

The Mission, San Francisco
January 10, 2014

Ofrenda

San Francisco, California

una ofrenda
sagrada es
nuestro barrio

en el Día
de los Muertos
cada año

la Misión
se convierte
en un altar –

cada uno
de nosotros
es una flor

una vela
prendida
en las calles

que recorremos
siguiendo
13 estandartes

13 *tonalli*
13 animales
nahuales guías

invocamos
los cuatro vientos
desde cuatro esquinas

nuestro barrio
la Misión
es un altar

colectivo
rebosante de
paz y armonía

2 de noviembre de 2011

Offering

San Francisco, California

our barrio
is a sacred
offering

on the Day
of the Dead
every year

the Mission
turns into
an altar –

each of us
turns into
a flower

a lit
candle
on the streets

we walk
following
13 standard bearers

13 *tonalli*
13 guiding
animal spirits

we invoke
the four winds
from four corners

the Mission
our barrio
is a collective

altar
overflowing with
peace and harmony

November 2, 2011

Invocación	Invocation
mi mano izquierda:	my left hand:
es el Este – el Fuego – me pinto todo rojo para recibir el Sol	is the East – Fire – I paint myself all red to welcome the Sun
mi mano derecha:	my right hand:
es el Norte – la Tierra – me visto de blanco al invocar los ancestros	is the North – Earth – I dress in white to invoke our ancestors
mi pie izquierdo:	my left foot:
es el Sur – el Agua – me pongo una corona amarilla de girasoles	is the South – Water – I put on a yellow crown made of sunflowers
mi pie derecho:	my right foot:
es el Oeste – el Viento – gracias le doy al manto negro de la noche	is the West – Wind – I give thanks to the black mantle of the night
mi cara está en el centro:	my face is at the center:
de mi boca salen floricantos a las cuatro direcciones de la Tierra	from my mouth flowersongs spring to the four directions of the Earth
2 de noviembre de 2011	*November 2, 2011*

Agirt

mo lámh chlé:

An tOirthear – Tine
cuirim dath dearg orm féin
chun fáiltiú roimh an nGrian

mo lámh dheas:

Tuaisceart – an Domhan
cuirim dath dearg orm féin
chun ár sinsir a ghairm

mo chos chlé:

an Deisceart – Uisce
cuirim coróin bhuí orm féin
de lusanna gréine

mo chos dheas:

an tIarthar – Gaoth –
gabhaim buíochas le cumhdach
dubh na hoíche

tá mo ghnúis sa lár:

bláthaíonn amhráin
as mo bhéal i dtreo
haird

Irish (Gaelic) translation by Gabriel Rosenstock

Iluminaciones

en el Solsticio Invernal
en la Misión de San Juan
Bautista, California

tras el amanecer
en el Solsticio Invernal
Papá Sol envía

un rayo de luz
a través de una ventana
de esta vieja misión

situada al filo
de la falla de San Andrés
de California –

los corazones son tambores
los ojos se centran en esta luz
las lenguas oran palomas

cuando Papá Sol entra
por los portones abiertos
cubriendo el pasillo

bendiciendo con su luz
el sacro altar dorado
y a todos los feligreses

iluminaciones –
misiones en comunión
con Mamá Tierra

con Papá Sol
con bendiciones y venia
de abuelos nativos

21 de diciembre de 2011

Illuminations

on Winter Solstice Day
at the San Juan Bautista
Mission, California

after daybreak
on the Winter Solstice
Father Sun sends

a ray of light
through a window
of this old mission

perched at the edge
of the San Andreas quake fault
in California –

hearts are drums
eyes focus on this light
tongues recite prayer doves

when Father Sun enters
through the open double doors
covering the long aisle

blessing with his light
the golden sacred altar
and all parishioners

illuminations –
missions in communion
with Mother Earth

with Father Sun
with blessings and consent
of native grandpas

December 21, 2011

Summer Solstice
In Teotihuacan

I

Teotihuacan –
Pyramid of the Sun – Earth
Mirror of Heavens

Teotihuacan –
Pirámide del Sol – Espejo
Terrenal del Cielo

Teotihuacan –
Pirimid na Gréine – Scáthán
Neimhe ar Talamh

II

like pilgrims we come
all dressed in white like clouds
on the Summer Solstice

como peregrinos
de blanco como nubes
el Solsticio de Verano

tagaimid inár n-oilithrigh dúinn
róbaí bána orainn ar nós néalta –
Grianstad an tSamhraidh

III

we all are one –
stones forming a pyramid –
branches of the same tree

todos somos uno –
piedras de una pirámide –
ramas de un mismo árbol

is aon sinn go léir –
clocha pirimide –
géaga crainn

IV

Pyramid of the Sun –
great collective dream –
vision mountain

Pirámide del Sol –
gran sueño colectivo –
monte visionario

Pirimid na Gréine –
Comhaisling ollmhór –
sliabh na dtaibhreamh

V

*in Xochitonatiuh –
nican xochitl in cuicatl
in ixtli in yollotl*

o, new Flower Sun –
you bring us flowersongs
to our faces and hearts

oh nuevo Sol Flor –
nos traes floricantos
al rostro y corazón

ó, a Ghrianbhláth nua
tugann tú bláthamhráin
dár n-aghaidh is dár gcroí

VI

Sixth Sun – Flower Sun –
new era making us all
bloom as flowers

Sexto Sol – Sol Flor –
nueva era haciéndonos
a todos florecer

Séú Grian – Grianbhláth
ré nua a chuireann cách
ag bláthú inár bhflóis dúinn

June 21, 2012

Irish (Gaelic) translation by Gabriel Rosenstock

Altar en el desierto

este no es
un poema
sino un altar

en el desierto
para ánimas
en pena

perdidas
cruzando
el desierto

buscando
una mejor
vida

hallando
una muerte
súbita

rebozantes
de plena vida
y sueños

con familias
pendientes
todavía

esperando
su seguro
retorno

estas no
son palabras
sino flores

doradas del Sol
cempasúchiles
en floreros

tazas
de chocolate
pan de muerto

velas prendidas
columnas
elevándose

danzando
de humo
de salvia y copal

ofrendas
para incontables
migrantes

muertos
intentando cruzar
la frontera

calaveritas
sin nombre
sin tumba

que
encuentren
un camino

a la Tierra
Prometida
a todos

desde
el principio
de los Tiempos

que
en el desierto
descansen en paz

que
sus familias
los restituyan

a la vida
con sus risas
lágrimas y todo

rescatándolos
del olvido
más cruel

este Día
de los Muertos
y ¡cada día!

27 de octubre de 2012

Desert Altar

this is
not a poem
but an altar

in the desert
for wandering
spirits

lost
crossing
the desert

looking
for a better
life

finding
sudden
death

full
of life
and dreams

with families
worrying
still

hoping
for their safe
return

these are
not words
but golden

flowers of the Sun
marigolds
in vases

cups
of chocolate
sweet breads

lit candles
columns
of sage

and copal
smoke raising
dancing

offerings
for countless
dead migrants

dead
trying to cross
the border

bones
without name
without grave

may
you find
your way

to the Land
Promised
to all

from
the beginning
of Time

may
you rest in peace
in the desert

may
your *familias*
restore you

to life
with laughter
tears and all

rescuing you
from cruelest
oblivion

this Day
of the Dead
and every day!

October 27, 2012

Iluminando oscuras noches	Illuminating Dark Nights
en total oscuridad – que haya luz	amid total darkness – let there be light
luz dulce luz fogosa luz amorosa	sweet light fiery light loving light
luz vuelta tibio aliento cantos prendidos	light turned warm breath glowing songs
brasas vivas iluminando oscuras noches –	live embers illuminating dark nights –
que haya luz en completa oscuridad	let there be light amid total darkness
15 de diciembre de 2013	*December 15, 2013*

¡Viva la vida!

abajo los muros
que nos separan
y nos agobian

abajo las cercas
que arruinan paisajes
y horizontes

abajo los portones
que permanecen
cerrados bajo llave

basta de cerrojos
aldabas, candados
postigos, cadenas

basta de dogmas
tabúes, prejuicios
y suposiciones

basta de verdades
a medias, mentiras
y falsedades

viva el aire libre
fresco sin medidor
del monte, del mar

vivan los pajáros
y las mariposas
sin fronteras

vivan los delfines
que alto retozan
llenos de alegría

¡abajo la muerte!
¡viva la vida
que a todo da vida!

31 de julio de 2012

Long Live Life!

down with walls
separating us
and oppressing us

down with fences
ruining landscapes
and horizons

down with gates
that remain locked up
under key

no more padlocks
deadbolts, latches
bars or chains

enough of dogmas
taboos, prejudices
or presumptions

no more half-
truths, white lies
or falsehoods

hooray free fresh
mountain and sea air
without a meter

way to go birds
and borderless
butterflies

bravo dolphins
tossing themselves high
in the air out of joy

down with death!
long live good life
giving out life to all!

July 31, 2012

147

Oh Luna llena – Canto inmemorial

al mirar la Luna llena tras el tifón Yolanda
en las Filipinas antes del Solsticio Invernal de 2013

oh Luna llena
rosa mística
celestial

un niño
levanta
la mano

queriendo
alcanzarte
acariciarte

lleno
de sueños
ilusiones

oh Luna llena
espejo marino
del Sol

ahora
un canoso
escriba

levanta
su vista
su pluma

implorando
tu luz guía
en la oscuridad

oh Luna llena
tierna madre
de la noche

consuela
al niño
huérfano

que llora
al ver tu faz
en las Filipinas

tras perderlo
todo en el Tifón
Yolanda

oh Luna llena
hermana fiel
de la Tierra

todos somos
hijos tuyos
también

cada uno
parte singular
del mismo

gran sueño
inmemorial
de la humanidad

17 de diciembre de 2013

O Full Moon – Immemorial Chant

*looking at the full Moon after Typhoon Yolanda
in the Philippines before the Winter Solstice of 2013*

o full Moon
mystic rose
of the sky

a child
raises
his hand

wishing
to reach you
caress you

filled with
illusions
dreams

o full Moon
sea mirror
of the Sun

now
a grey-haired
scribe

raises
his sight
his writing pen

imploring
your guiding light
in the darkness

o full Moon
tender Mother
of the night

console
the orphaned
kid weeping

upon seeing
your face
in the Philippines

after losing all
to Typhoon
Yolanda

o full Moon
faithful sister
of the Earth

we are all
your children
as well

each of us
a singular part
of the same

immemorial
big dream
of humanity

December 17, 2013

149

Un Solsticio – Una Tierra

en la noche más larga del Hemisferio del Norte	en la noche más larga del Hemisferio del Norte	en el día más largo del Hemisferio del Sur
la Luna llora todavía en las costas isleñas de las Filipinas	el Sol en Stonehenge nos besa a todos en la frente –	el Sol danza en los Picos Dedos de los Andes
tras la gran calamidad humana debido al Tifón Haiyan/Yolanda	alzamos la vista y el corazón para mirar al Sol más al Sur	y sobre las piedras de cóndores y serpientes de Machu Picchu –
mas en solidaridad surgen contribuciones poéticas/artísticas	de todo el año el colibrí volador/el Sol en Chichen Itzá –	¿solsticio de invierno o verano? la Tierra es una – todos de veras somos uno
de poetas, escritores, artistas de las Filipinas y del mundo entero	el Sol al atardecer marca la Espiral de Piedra en el Cañón de Chaco –	cuando lloras te alegras, todos lloramos todos nos alegramos
preciosa mariposas deseosas de curar todas las heridas de cuerpo y alma	en los brazos de la noche abrazamos la esperanza real	una humanidad un solsticio una Tierra

21 de diciembre de 2013

One Solstice – One Earth

in the longest night
of the Northern
Hemisphere

the Moon still weeps
over the island shores
of the Philippines

after the great human
calamity due to Typhoon
Haiyan/Yolanda

yet in solidarity
come out poetic/artistic
surges, outpourings

from poets, writers
artists from the Philippines
and all over the world

precious butterflies
wishing to heal all body
and soul wounds

in the longest night
of the Northern
Hemisphere

the Sun at Stonehenge
kisses us all
on our foreheads –

we raise our sight
and heart facing
the lowest Sun

of the year to greet
the hummingbird/Sun
at Chichen Itzá –

the Sun at dusk
frames the Stone Spiral
at Chaco Canyon –

in the arms of night
we embrace
true hope

in the longest day
of the Southern
Hemisphere

the Sun dances
on the Finger Peaks
of the Andes

and over the condor
and serpent stones
of Machu Picchu –

Winter or Summer
Solstice? the Earth is one –
we are truly one

when you weep
rejoice, we all weep
we all rejoice with you

one humankind
one solstice
one Earth

December 21, 2013

¿Qué es un poeta?

en homenaje a Víctor Martínez
(1954-2011)

una pregunta
rumeando como gato
en total oscuridad

un monje tenaz
que prendiéndoles
fuego a las palabras

una presencia
perenne que desafía
cualquier ausencia

una puerta abierta
sin cerrojos, sin llaves
que encara al mar

se inmola
para darle al mundo
algo de su luz

una conversación
entre la vida y la muerte
que no tiene fin

una lámpara
encendida durante
toda la noche

una mirada
que no deja de velar
por los demás

una mariposa
un colibrí en el aire –
un ser y no estar

una voz sin voz
que es alegría y
enojo a la vez

una honestidad
tan feroz hasta dejar
desnuda a la verdad

cuando un poeta muere
sus poemas florecen
en nuestro corazón

Ciudad de Guatemala
20 de febrero de 2011

What Is A Poet?

in homage of Victor Martínez
(1954–2011)

a question roaming
here and there like a cat
in complete darkness

a persistent monk
who in keeping
words lit turns

a perennial presence
that confronts
any given absence

a door opened
– no lock no key –
to face the sea

himself into
a living torch
lighting the world

a conversation
without end
between life and death

a lamp
that burns
from dusk to dawn

an unending gaze
keeping vigil over
the fate of others

a butterfly flitting
a hummingbird hovering–
here but never bound

a voiceless voice
that is at once joy
and rage

an honesty so fierce –
no ceasing till it gets
at the naked truth

when a poet dies
his poems unfurl
inside our chest

Guatemala City
February 20, 2014
English translation by Francisco Aragón with the poet

Danza de las mariposas	Butterfly Dance
esta noche me pongo	I'm doing tonight
a bailar la antigua danza	the ancient dance
de las mariposas	of the butterflies
extiendo los brazos	spreading my arms
moviéndolos como alas	flapping them like wings
de mariposas en vuelo	of butterflies in flight
como mi abuelita	just as my grandma
una vez me enseñó	once told me as a kid
de niño invocando:	invoking the chant:
in papalotl	*in papalotl*
in tonatiuh	*in tonatiuh*
in tlanextia…	*in tlanextia…*
oh mariposa	o butterfly
que siempre	may your Sun
brille tu Sol…	forever shine…
está oscuro y frío	it's dark and cold
solo bajo la lluvia	I'm weeping alone
empiezo a llorar	in the rain
oh por nuestras	o for our sisters
hermanas, las mariposas	the monarch
monarcas…	butterflies…
la más pequeña	the smallest
criatura es de las más	of creatures is really
grandes en verdad…	one of the greatest…
29 de enero de 2014	*January 29, 2014*

154

Sin sentido	Senseless
oímos	we hear
pero no	but don't
escuchamos	listen
vemos	we see
pero no	but don't
entendemos	get it
hablamos	we speak
pero solo	but only
balbuceamos	mumble
sabemos	we learn
pero no	but don't
sentimos –	feel –
el miedo	the fear
las lágrimas	the tears
las muertes	the deaths
de otros	of others
ya no nos	no longer
conmueven	move us
debemos estar	we must be
en Gaza	in Gaza
Palestina	Palestine
o en la frontera	or on the US –
entre EE.UU.	Mexico
y México	border

21 de julio de 2014   *July 21, 2014*

Frontera

herida
abierta
sin cicatrizar

espina
clavada
en el corazón

Muro
de Lamentos
para familias

fantasía
pesadilla
desilusión

refugio
purgatorio
infierno

para miles
tumba sin
demarcación

oh desierto
abrazando
al cielo

oh partición
del alma de
la humanidad

8 de agosto de 2014

Border

open
bleeding
wound

thorn
piercing
the heart

Wall
of Laments
for families

fantasy
nightmare
delusion

refuge
purgatory
hell

unmarked
tomb for
thousands

o desert
embracing
the sky

o partition
of the soul
of humanity

August 8, 2014

Tankas sin fronteras

oh imagínate
el mundo sin fronteras
toda la gente
soñando, volando libres
como mariposas monarcas

los poetas caen
como estrellas fugaces –
dan luz al cielo
brevemente a los ojos
y para siempre al alma

27 de julio de 2014

olivos en todos
los corazones – hojitas
de olivo en el pico
de la Paloma de la Paz –
olivos vencen guerras

31 de julio de 2014

oh bayonetas
del mundo sin corazón
rodeando a niños
mujeres en el Monte
Sinyar, Gaza, la frontera sur

9 de agosto de 2014

fronteras se borran
con el poder encantador
del cilantro verde –
¡oh sabor conquistador
en salsa y guacamole!

11 de agosto de 2014

Borderless Tankas

o imagine
this world without borders
all the people dreaming
flying free everywhere
as monarch butterflies

poets come down
as shooting stars –
they lighten the sky
so briefly the eyes
and forever the soul

July 27, 2014

olive trees in all
the hearts – some olive
leaves in the beak
of the Dove of Peace –
olive trees vanquish wars

July 31, 2014

o bayonets
of this heartless world
surrounding children
women in Mount Sinjar
Gaza, the southern border

August 9, 2014

all borders disappear
with the thrilling power
of green cilantro –
o conquering taste of fresh
salsa and guacamole!

August 11, 2014

el mundo es ancho
y ajeno – y aún así
las flores florecen
y nunca pierden rumbo
las aves ni mariposas

12 de agosto de 2014

the world is wide
and alien – and yet flowers
keep on blooming
and birds and butterflies
never get off their flight course

August 12, 2014

que mariposas
ballenas, siempre rijan
aire, tierra y mar

1 de enero de 2014

may butterflies, whales
forever rule the air
the land, the sea

January 1, 2014

About Francisco

Francisco X. Alarcón, award-winning Chicano poet and educator, was born in Los Angeles, grew up in Guadalajara, Mexico, and now lives in Davis, where he teaches at the University of California. He is the author of twelve volumes of poetry, including *Canto hondo / Deep Song* (University of Arizona Press, 2015), *Ce • Uno • One: Poems for the New Sun* (Swan Scythe Press, 2010), *From the Other Side of Night / Del otro lado de la noche: New and Selected Poems* (University of Arizona Press, 2002), *Sonnets to Madness and Other Misfortunes* (Creative Arts Book Company, 2001), *No Golden Gate for Us* (Pennywhistle Press, 1993), *Snake Poems: An Aztec Invocation* (Chronicle Books, 1992), *Of Dark Love* (Moving Parts Press, 1991 and 2001), and *Body in Flames* (Chronicle Books, 1990).

Francisco is the author of four acclaimed books of bilingual poems for children on the seasons of the year originally published by Children's Book Press, now an imprint of Lee & Low Books: *Laughing Tomatoes and Other Spring Poems* (1997), *From the Bellybutton of the Moon and Other Summer Poems* (1998), *Angels Ride Bikes and Other Fall Poems* (1999), and *Iguanas in the Snow and Other Winter Poems* (2001). He has published two other bilingual books for children with Lee & Low Books: *Poems to Dream Together* (2005) and *Animal Poems of the Iguazú* (2008). He has received numerous literary awards and prizes for his works, including the American Book Award, the Pen Oakland Josephine Miles Award, the Chicano Literary Prize, the Fred Cody Lifetime Achievement Award, the Jane Adams Honor Book Award, and several Pura Belpré Honor Book Awards by the American Library Association. In 1993, he co-founded *Los Escritores del Nuevo Sol / Writers of the New Sun*, a collective of writers based in Sacramento, California. He is the creator of the Facebook page "Poets Responding to SB 1070."

Press Producers

Friend of the Press
- Heartfelt Thanks

Andrea Robinson
Jeanne Andrews
Maina le Glatin
Kiirsti Peterson

Paul Dolinsky
Anne Whitehouse
Jocelyn A. Avendano
Anonymous

Supporter of the Press
- Deepest Gratitude

Jodi Dills
Dick Keis
Mary Ellen Wilson
Carmen Calatayud
Emmy Pérez
Linda Wilson

Lynn Merrill
Marta I Galindo
Chris Hoffman
John Juan Adams
Anonymous

Sponsor of the Press
- Profound Appreciation

Nancy Aidé González
Don Cellini
Andrea Romero
Thomas Gayton
Ayda Lucero Fleck

JC Allen
Todd Coates
Francisco Aragón
Beth Pratt
Anonymous

Patron of the Press
- Keen Affection

Joyce Downs
Anne Apfel
Martha Benavides
Graciela B. Ramírez
Odilia Galván Rodríguez
Priscilla Del Bosque-Schouten

Sally Andrade
JoAnn Anglin
Jacquelyn Marie
Ulla Hamilton
Mónica Lozano
Anonymous

Press Producers

I would like to thank all of those who worked on and participated in our campaign to raise finances for *Borderless Butterflies: Earth Haikus and Other Poems / Mariposas sin fronteras: Haikus terrenales y otros poemas* by Francisco X. Alarcón. Thanks to James Downs, Devon Peterson, and Joyce Downs. A special thanks to Francisco for the opportunity to work on this beautiful book; to Manuela Vargas Fernández for her fine video work and Javier Pinzón for his hospitality. And of course, thanks to all of these people who contributed so generously to this effort.

Small poetry press publishing is a joy to do but certainly costs money and these Producers, like in any artistic effort, are the ones who make it possible.
Thank you!
— John Peterson, Publisher

CPSIA information can be obtained
at www.ICGtesting.com
Printed in the USA
FSOW02n1128161016
26201FS